*In Couch to Kilimanjaro, She[...]
into her gripping real-life [...]
able to identify with. The [...]
well written and draws the re[...]er in. Though filled with
some painful stories, Sheralyn offers real hope in the
midst of life's tough challenges.
We wholeheartedly recommend this book.*

**Steve and Esther Uppal, Senior Leaders at All Nations,
Wolverhampton**

*A real person. A real challenge. In the face of failure both
on the mountain and in daily life, Sheralyn faces up to her
personal battles. A fight for her own sanity, defeating her
own fears and insecurities. A fight for others, too — a
struggle for justice. Each of us have our Kilimanjaro's. Each
of us have our mountains to climb. This book will
be the inspiration you need to keep going.*

**Ralph Turner, Christian Author and writer of Mountain
Climbing for Beginners (mountain50.blogspot.com)**

*Couch to Kilimanjaro is a great read for everyone.
Sheralyn does an excellent job of speaking candidly about
overcoming challenges. Right from the beginning, the
brutal honesty of the stories captures your attention,
making you want to read more. We were captivated by
this book and could imagine the black leather couch and
the tears, defeat, joy, laughter and hope that came
through as Sheralyn shared her life with us. The end of
chapter challenges are a particularly good addition.It is
an excellent choice for anyone wanting to make that
journey from their proverbial 'Couch to Kilimanjaro'!*

**Pastor Henry and Dr Rachael Ita, Senior Pastors,
New Life Church, Derby**

*The mountains we experience in life are loaded with both exhaustion and excitement. The parallels between a near-death experience on a physical mountain in Africa and the emotional mountains of loss of loved ones and relationships, depression and addiction are exposed in abject humility by Sheralyn in this short exposé. Just as the darkness, thin air and perils on the physical mountain parallel challenge and tragedy in everyday life, so, too, do the joys and triumphs shared with others on the trail. My Bestie, Sheralyn, brought me back to the mountain top and the darkest moments all while purposefully acknowledging our Lord and Saviour in her telling of this powerful testimony of hope!*

**LtCol David 'T-Bone' Trombly USMC (Ret), Author, Speaker, Chaplain and Sheralyn's Kilimanjaro climbing partner**

*The beauty of someone sharing their story is that it shows us more of our own as we recognise our shared humanity. I certainly experienced this dynamic through these pages and I felt as though I was sitting on Sheralyn's 'black leather couch' listening to her sharing about life and loss in a very real and raw way. A great reminder that a moment of crisis provides an opportunity for self-reflection leading to the possibility of gaining fresh perspective on the whole of life's journey.*

**Simon Shaw, Spiritual Coach**

*Life can be great at sending trials, tests and a fair few challenges along the way; all of these moments help to shape who we are and strengthen the deepest areas of our hearts.*
*In Sheralyn's case, this was both a literal mountain and also the mountains of dealing with loss. I encourage you to read this book to be strengthened in your journey ,Whether that journey is fighting slavery and exploitation — like One By One — or your own freedom from addictions and anxiety. Have the courage to take that first step and move into all that you were created to be.*
**Becky Murray, Founder and CEO, One By One**
**www.onebyone.net**

*As you will discover, I first met Sheralyn at an evangelism training course that I had been invited to lead at New Life Church, Derby. She was enthusiastic, honest and passionate for justice. Her compassion for hurting people shone through. In many ways, that is Sheralyn's story...it is honest, gutsy and full of life. God has taken her from a place of brokenness to an overcoming life — and she is determined to help and lift as many people as she can in the unfolding journey of her life with Him.*
**Jonathan Conrathe Founder and Director, Mission24**

# COUCH TO
# KILIMANJARO

To Nicky,

Be blessed and inspired -

Thank you so much for all you
do at Restore.

Love and hugs

Shealy xxx    6/12/22

**PublishU**

www.PublishU.com

# Dedication

To Mum and Dad, Michelle and Marie — my family

Mum and Dad, you gave me the resilience, the inspiration and the training to climb any mountains in life — you are my heroes.

To my lovely sisters: we were made from formidable stuff. I love you both so much, miss you Marie and thank you Michelle for your never-ending texts, encouragement and support.

# Contents

Throughout this book, the pictures of the experience shared can be found on the Couch to Kilimanjaro Facebook page:

https://www.facebook.com/Couch-to-Kilimanjaro

You can also connect and share your experiences of the book.

Email: couchtokilimanjaro@yahoo.co.uk

# Thank You

Thank you to my New Life Church family for encouraging and supporting me throughout this journey. This book was conceptualised during lockdown, and I would like to say a special thanks to the following people who supported its writing and journey with me during that time. Thank you to Pastors Henry and Rachel Ita, Mary and Bill, Cathy and Kerry, Liz and Dave, Kit and Peter and Rosie. I could fill a book with the names of so many of the other folk who have stood with me and prayed throughout this journey. This book would not be in print at all without your constant reassurance and support.

I'd give a special thank you to Tim Nelson, who led us on a most amazing trek up Kilimanjaro. I have never known a leader that can multitask so well. He looked after each one of us in consultation with our chief guide. He remembered major donors and sponsorship tasks, letters from home, everything he needed to do at the summit whilst being oxygen starved. I would not have got far without the support of Tim in both the fundraising and the challenge. A total legend and huge inspiration.

I have mentioned some specific people in my story but all 22 people who attempted that mountain deserve a mention of special thanks: to Tim, T-Bone, Greg, Tod, Geoff, Jen, Harriet, Hunter, Ben, Jacob, Andrew, Andy J, Ernie, Lou, AD, Andy W, Zak W, Jim, Alicia, Dom and Tom. As you will read, without the amazing and encouraging Extreme Challenge Team, I would not have made it as far as I did.

When I was low, they put up with my singing and when I needed a hug, they provided. One day soon we will meet again...maybe Everest Base Camp next time? By helicopter maybe!

Massive thank you to Jonathan Conrathe and the Mission24 team — I'm truly inspired by Impact Week and beyond. If I had not stepped out with you all, I have no doubt that stepping out to climb a mountain would still be a pipe dream. Love the mission and love joining you when I am able to sharing the good news!

A very special thanks to Ralph Turner, whose honest feedback and proofreading meant this book is now in a place where it will (hopefully) inspire others. Your honesty with me was amazing — if you write a book, I recommend Ralph as the most amazing proofreader ever! Complete with an exclamation mark just for you Ralph.

A massive shout out, too, to Kandoo Adventures who provided an excellent ten-man guide crew and forty-eight porters — fifty-eight people in total to assist us. It took that number of people for the twenty-two person attempt to climb Kilimanjaro: twenty-two of us attempted it, eighteen of us made the summit. It would not have been possible without the dedication and hard work from Kandoo Adventures team.

And finally, a massive shout out to Matt Bird. If I had not completed the 'writing my book' course, you would not be reading this book. The mentoring support of Matt and the team, mean we are here now. I absolutely recommend this course — we all have a book in us!

# Foreword

For anyone who has been living a life on autopilot, and never attempted anything beyond the ordinary, this book could be a motivator for you to get off your 'blessed assurance' and reach out to a life you only dreamed of. Your faith may have been tested, but you must not give up. I believe this book will challenge you to reflect on what has happened to you and what you will do next.

It may take a 'jolt' to get out of stuck, like the one Sheralyn had when her sister passed away. For others, it may be another event. It may be a growing awareness that you need to change your status quo. We only have one life and we must make the most of every moment. Losing loved ones can happen to us all at some point in our lives; and through that tragedy what will the impact have us do?

In writing her story, Sheralyn has helped us understand the journey that she has taken through life, with its defining moments, and at the same time, the journey that she has taken to tackle and incredible feet of climbing Mount Kilimanjaro.

I had the privilege to be on the journey to Tanzania prior to the pandemic with Sheralyn and a team of 20 others. The aim was to raise money to help bring us closer to ending modern slavery across the world. It was a precious group of people, and we still talk regularly. We often share WhatsApp messages in the group.

In fundraising terms, Sheralyn is spoken of in legendary status as she had so many individual donations for her fundraising page. She brings so much personality and life into everything she does. For many who travelled on that trip, it was a life-defining time. I have met many people and spoken about how their lives pivoted as a result of the changes they have made; they are now enjoying the new life they have discovered.

Sheralyn is a passionate person and for six months she wore a fundraising t-shirt every day and encouraged everyone she could to donate. She even spoke to strangers on the plane to Tanzania and managed to influence others to get involved. I believe that the efforts she has shown in leaving a legacy in remembrance of her sister is incredibly powerful. This world needs more people like Sheralyn!

As you read this book, I hope you will see yourself through the mirror that Sheralyn holds up and encourages you to dream impossible dreams. I'm so glad to count Sheralyn as a friend and honoured that she would ask me to be a part of her story and this book.

**Tim Nelson, Chief Executive Officer, Hope for Justice and Slave-Free Alliance**

# Preface

The date is 3rd June, 2015. I am bereft! I have come from the bed to the black leather couch and am wallowing in grief and pity. I have put on my 'go to' films. First I watch A Few Good Men, a story of injustice — just what I feel right now. I get to the scene where Jack Nicholson screams 'you can't handle the truth' to Tom Cruise. Jack Nicholson is right! The tears just keep flowing.

I grab a glass of red wine I have just opened — plenty of time to be too drunk to face the next day — and swig. There is a full bottle of Jack Daniels in the cabinet, I have at least 20 cigarettes and I am wallowing, wallowing, wallowing...

SHERALYN PATTISON

# Chapter 1
# Emergency Stations

*It's the 27th October, 2019. I am feeling ill ... I am back at camp having attempted to summit the mountain – the mighty Kilimanjaro. My guide measured my O2 saturation ('O2') again and it was sixty-three percent. There had been no recovery at all. My guide was starting to get concerned. It was the middle of the night and pitch black.*

*The terrain is rocky, icy, snowy. Walking anywhere is just not possible. I am helped to my tent by the porters and collapse on my back.*

*I am exhausted and defeated. I am feeling at my lowest point. If I'm honest, I was hoping and praying I would make it through the night and meet the morning. I can still see the tent now. I was alone in our camp. I couldn't hear any guides or porters and I knew my O2 was low. Thankfully, I had no clue then of the importance of O2 saturation in the blood! I cried and cried and cried, defeated, until I fell to sleep.*

*I am not sure what time it was when I awoke but my guide was measuring my O2 again. It was still sixty-three percent. He left me and said I needed to get dressed. He would be back again in a few minutes.*

*My guide came back and measured my O2 once again. Still sixty-three percent! I felt so rubbish and everything zapped my energy. I had a massive headache and was struggling to breathe. I felt like I was drunk.*

*I described how I felt, and I can remember what the guide said as clear as if it was yesterday: 'We need to get you off this mountain.' Funnily enough, I agreed! He instructed me to pack everything as quickly as possible and meet him at the mess tent. Again, he measured my O2. It was still sixty-three percent...we were in dangerous territory.*

*At this point, I started to wonder how on earth I got into this position; I was slipping in and out of conscious thought. I had the most awful headache. Every movement took my breath away...how had I got here? The feeling reminded me of a day long ago. I was 17..*

---

## College Dayz

Attending A-Level college, halfway through the school year. I was hanging out with a group of friends in the common room. They began passing a Coca-Cola can around. Not knowing what was in it, I took it and had massive gulp. I nearly choked and my throat was on fire. All my friends laughed and then informed me it was single malt whisky! Now I knew what I was drinking, I carried on. (I must confess here that I later told my parents that I didn't know what was in the can, but ... well, I did!)

I continued to drink. And drink. Laughter and confidence flowed. After the can was finished, we debated who looked the oldest and most innocent — the consensus was it was me. In hindsight, I think everyone else in the group had been caught for underage drinking before and I hadn't.

We marched down to the local supermarket and, with a confidence that can only come through drinking neat whisky, I picked up another bottle of single malt: Glenfiddich. I only knew the brand because my dad enjoyed a tipple! I must have looked like an expert to the checkout staff as they didn't even question my age. Bonus! No ID required! We went back to the common room and continued drinking right through the afternoon.

I don't remember much after returning from the supermarket, but we must have drunk at least a quarter bottle each. The next thing I knew, I was on a changing room floor with a paramedic next to me. I'm sure this was not a pretty sight or smell. It was a scene of carnage with some serious vomiting that I didn't investigate further, but it must have been a challenge for anyone sober. That poor cleaner who followed me in there!

When the ambulance appeared on site (to this day I do not know who called it) the Principal had been notified. When I say notified, I later found out that he panicked when the 'blues and twos' appeared outside the front of the college building. On finding out who the sick pupil was, he called my emergency contacts — Mum and Dad. I don't remember getting from the changing rooms to the Principal's office, but I did get there. When I entered the office, there was Dad. Too drunk to see the look on his face, I just burst into tears and started apologising. I remember Dad had to help me get into the front of the car as I was still very drunk. I must have smelled nicely of Eau-de-whisky and vomit.

My Dad had agreed to collect my Mum from the church where she led a Rainbow Guide pack. This was the late

80s and mobile phones had just been invented and were still the exclusive property of yuppies. Dad had no way of notifying Mum of what to expect. When Dad arrived at the church, Mum let him know she had offered to give two of the other leaders a lift home. Mum and Dad were mortified at having to explain why their youngest daughter was subconscious in the front of the car, smelling rather interesting! Back home, it was straight upstairs to bed.

I had a cleaning job to do the next day and Dad took great delight in waking me up at 7am to get me started. The cleaning didn't go well: I fell asleep on the bed. If my parents were not praying for me before this event in my life, I am certain they did afterwards. That day was my first experience of a hangover. My head was so sore and not dissimilar to how I was feeling at the top of that mountain...

---

*The guide had given me some fluids and we had started to hike out of camp for the emergency descent. The terrain was slippery and snowy, and I was not recovering at all. I was clinging onto the guide for dear life! We began to trek down to the emergency station. By a mighty miracle, I was still able to move but leaned heavily on the guide to balance and steady myself as I put one foot in front of the other. The O2 reading was still sixty-three percent. My oxygen intake had seemingly not improved at all. I felt rubbish but was still moving. I am no medic, but I am fairly sure that with those readings, I should not have been walking. I prayed more earnestly than I had ever prayed in my life to get back home safely — to be able to enjoy the black leather couch once again...*

---

## The Journey on the Couch begins

The black leather couch had been purchased in an unsteady period of married life. My ex-husband Iain and I had moved from Huddersfield to Derby. We had enjoyed five or six years of being 'DINKYs' (Double Income, No Kids Yet) and this had continued. Iain had advanced in his career and I in mine. We had decided to buy a house locally and settle, having rented when we first moved. We found the house, had a mortgage offer and the buying process was well underway. At that time, one of my colleagues and close friends developed sarcoma, a form of cancer, and passed away ... at 38 years of age. This hit me hard. His wife relied heavily on me during that time.

Then, I lost my job. I can honestly say that someone was watching out for us during that time. I interviewed for another job within weeks and was offered it. The new job was significantly more money and much better terms.

So began a new house and a new job — things were getting brighter.

At this time, we decided to buy a new couch. We dutifully went to the never-ending DFS sale and found some really comfy black leather couches. There were two of them, one a three-seater and a two-seater. During the few years prior buying the house, I had made many mistakes in our marriage. We were drifting apart.

It was after the purchase of this house — and just one day sitting on our new black leather couch — that I decided to try harder, put the mistakes aside make a go of our marriage.

I was going to stop playing at marriage. In 2005, six years after Iain and I had got married, we were finally settling into life together. Those first six years were difficult, and I felt the future was going to be better — different! That black leather couch meant success and a bright future was ahead.

---

*After a short while the guide seated me on a rock and went back to camp. To this day, I have no idea why. He arrived back and measured my O2 saturation. Still sixty-three percent. Just to explain O2 saturation: at ground level O2 Saturation should be over ninety percent. Anything under that and hospital treatment is usually required. At altitude, O2 saturation under eighty percent is a concern. Anything under seventy-five percent and vital organs begin to shut down. My O2 being at the level it was really wasn't beneficial for long-term health! We continued our journey down to the emergency station.*

*Let me tell you about hydration and altitude: whilst climbing Kilimanjaro, the guides advise that you drink three litres of water every day. This has an inevitable consequence at any point in time! I am sure you can imagine that Shanks hasn't quite plumbed in toilets at every 100 yards up the mountain in this remote part of Tanzania. There are luxurious long drops at camps or, if you are blessed like we were, Portaloos in separate tents were also available. During any day of the climb though, it was time to experience the liberating feeling of that 'wild wee'! The guides would find some rocks or a tree to hide one's dignity (or what was left of it depending on the stage of the climb). This, however, was not always possible and did prove a problem when approaching the wheeled stretchers (gurneys) in the emergency rescue point. Dignity wasn't ever an issue for me ... my parents prepared me well!*

---

## Inflation Is Stripping Me Bare

In the late 70s, finances were a struggle for most working-class families. Inflation was going through the roof at around fourteen percent, taxes were rising, and it was becoming more difficult for any working family to make ends meet. iPads, Xboxes and mobile phones hadn't been invented yet. There were only three channels on the TV. We had to make our own entertainment — yes, we had to talk to each other!

Group entertainment with other families on the street and beyond was a way of passing the time. Mum and Dad were no exception to families that were struggling. One of my favourite entertainment activities was a fancy-dress competition at any and every street party or celebration going. We had the Queen's Silver Jubilee in 1977 and the marriage of Prince Charles to Princess Diana in 1981 amongst other celebrations.

Mum was ingenious with her fancy-dress costume-making skills.

My sisters had costumes made of tea bags, toilet rolls, old newspapers ... whatever Mum could invent and reuse became a costume. The most successful costume my Mum created was rather literally made of nothing. It was first used at some event to celebrate the Queen's Jubilee in 1977. The costume was me up on stage, stark naked. My dignity was covered with two pieces of cardboard, pinned together over my shoulders, like a billboard. The cardboard had written on it in big bold black letters 'Inflation is stripping me bare'. The costume caused much hilarity and won first prize almost every time it was wheeled out. At that age, I had no clue what the adults were laughing about; in my eyes, I was a winner doing something special!

---

*We arrived at the gurneys used for emergency evacuation. I asked the guide how long it was before there was any luxurious long drop and he confirmed my worst fears: it would be at least an hour. Those gurneys looked unsteady and not the most comfortable ... not the best when needing to go. I did what anyone would in the circumstances; I told the 12 male porters to turn around and walk for about fifty to one hundred yards. Let's face it, anyone who paraded nude with a sign at a talent show would not mind this lack of dignity!*

*The gurneys are one-wheeled metal stretchers that you are strapped into. They are situated just in front of the peak of Kilimanjaro. I saw my perfect summit picture opportunity with Mr Delicious (our cook), the porters and my guide. I was feeling much better and my O2 saturation at this point had moved to seventy percent. I saw my opportunity to get my 'summit' shot. I was strapped into the gurney inside my sleeping bag, the day pack behind my head as a pillow and my holdall at my feet to stop me rolling forward. I asked the porters to pose and there you have it, that was my 'summit' shot.*

*As we began our descent off the mountain, I was feeling rough and was not really aware at all of my surroundings. I was thinking about the descent that lay ahead and wished it had been like the waterslide Dad made in the garden when we were children...*

---

One of my all-time favourite memories as a child was that waterslide. Dad was just so creative. We had old municipal swings he had recommissioned in our garden, but we also had what was a municipal slide that had been dumped. Dad recycled it: he put a new metal slide on it and it became functional. We had a downhill, sloping back garden. Dad would tie a hose pipe at the very top of the slide. At the bottom, was a plastic sheet about three metres long. We positioned our rubbish bins at the bottom. The bottom was directly next to the brick wall of the side of the house. As a result, all the children in our neighbourhood had the most amazing waterslide for the hot summer days. (Back then, they seemed to exist in abundance!) If you had asked anybody in our neighbourhood about that slide, they would all remember it. It was just so brilliant and such good fun. Just a great creative, repurposed slide from Dad. I was hoping for a similar descent down this mountain.

*We began our descent. It wasn't like the waterslide ... it was bumpy. (Put 'Kilimanjaro Stretcher' into YouTube and watch the first video — an eye opener!) There was a reason that I had signed up for the Extreme Challenge and I will explain more later, but I had set myself a target of funds to raise at £10,000. I had not summited the mountain. When I left the village of Moshi for the climb, I had only raised £7,200. I was going to let all my supporters down; I had not completed the challenge. I hoped none of them wanted refunds! There were twenty-two of us completing the challenge and we had to raise a minimum of £5,000 each. I had achieved that but really wanted to honour my sister, Marie, and raise the rest. I drifted into the deepest thoughts as to how I had arrived on that mountain.*

# End of chapter challenge

In this first chapter, I have shared a couple of times where I made a fool of myself.

The first challenge here is to find some examples where you completely made a fool of yourself. Now, once you have remembered them, laugh at yourself. Write down these memories and when times get tough in your mountain, remember them. Laugh at those memories, let them bring a smile to your face. We all have a tendency to take life too seriously. Other people will not always see how important your mountain is to you.

If you can laugh at yourself and appreciate how wonderful an individual you are, you have the beginnings to be kind to yourself when looking at your own progress.

SHERALYN PATTISON

# Chapter 2
# Jolted!
# The Phone Call That
# Changed my Life

It was 31st July, 2009 — and I received a phone call I will never forget. Even now, as I write this, I recall exactly where I was.

I was driving my car around the neighbourhood. Iain and I were prepping to go away with friends for a combined stag and hen do at Center Parcs. I had just been to the local supermarket. Mum phoned and asked whether I was driving — very strange. I responded in the affirmative but that I was just round the corner from home. She seemed relieved.

The next words out of Mum's mouth shocked, stunned and took me aback: 'Marie is dead'.

Who, how, why, what, where, when?

Every question flashed through my mind and across my lips. No answers were to come until much later.

Marie had gone on holiday to Italy. Marie was now dead.

My parents knew little else. she died the day before. I knew all they knew.

It was Friday evening and there was little that could be done until Monday to find out more. In writing this, I feel the chilling words and circumstances even now, so many years later.

I opened the front door to the house and told Iain. I slumped down on the black leather couch in shock and disbelief. I didn't know what to do. I was supposed to be going away that weekend and having a party with my friends. I was in total shock. I didn't know whether to postpone. I didn't know whether to go around to my parents.

I just didn't know.

I was in shock. I was feeling shaken. I had no clue as to how to respond. All I could do was sit there on the black leather couch. Shocked. Devastated.

I hadn't spoken to Marie for six months. Every time I had tried to talk to her, she was drunk. She had been in an abusive marriage and then another abusive relationship and turned to alcohol. She told me so many horrific stories about the marriage when we managed to speak, but by then the marriage was over.

My hope was that she died painlessly.

Marie's life had been painful. She had lived with abuse and then her children were used as pawns in a battle for custody and control. The fight in court hurt both children. If you are a parent currently going through a battle with an ex-partner, please remember your children do not deserve to be used to hurt the other party, they will suffer for years if you do.

All children deserve to have both parents in their life no matter what adults think of each other.

It turns out that Marie died of a broken heart. Literally!

Back on the black leather couch, Iain was very supportive and would go wherever I wanted to go. I spoke to Mum and Dad again. They both advised nothing could be changed and that I should go away and see my friends that weekend. I would get support from them, too, so we decided to go. My parents were pragmatists and they knew that nothing practical could be done until the following Monday.

Iain and I decided to share the news only with the people in our chalet at Center Parcs. The stag and hen would not need to know until after the weekend. We would try and enjoy the time with our friends but I was morose that first evening at Center Parcs. I tried to put the situation to the back of my mind and help the future bride and groom enjoy their weekend. I'm pretty sure they didn't know until I informed them after the weekend.

On the Monday morning, we went to Mum and Dad's. I don't think I will ever forget walking into their house. I went straight to the kettle. That feeling of helplessness as I somehow forgot how to make a cup of tea — but that's what the shock did to me. I had managed all weekend to pretend it hadn't happened.

At that moment of walking into Mum and Dad's house, the reality of the circumstances hit me. Tears streamed down my face and I still didn't know how to put the kettle on.

That memory and that shock ... that feeling of loss and restlessness.

The bereft feeling of knowing that I wasn't going to see my sister again. And knowing that was it. THAT WAS IT. It was done. It was final. My prayer is that she is in heaven. Marie was 36 years old and had lived a troubled life. She'd married the wrong person and turned to alcohol to cope with the pain. And now...

## Italia and back

I cannot remember much of those next weeks after Marie's death. It was a constant blur of phone calls to the international funeral directors, legal processes, and insurance matters. Between Dad, Michelle (my eldest sister), and me, we navigated everything. The week after Marie died, we collected her few belongings from where she was staying. In and amongst them was a box full of paperwork. Marie's life was in that box. Her life had amounted to one box and a couple of bags.

Dad, Michelle, and I laid the paperwork out on the dining room table. We began the painstaking process of sorting through it. It took over three days. There were letters from years ago from creditors, from her previous mortgagee, all in envelopes that had never been opened. Marie had clearly been in trouble and just buried her head in the sand. She appeared not to have opened letters for years: bailiffs, debt collectors ... all just so sad.

We were there as a family and Marie just didn't reach out.

If you are reading this and you can relate, call someone (there is a list at the end of this book) don't bury your head. There is no shame in asking for help. It won't go away and you end up drowning.

There were so many debts. After all debts were paid and the funeral was settled, there was a total £3,000 left. It was halved and sent to Marie's children. It was so sad that a 36-year-old life had amounted to a collection of paper and a few clothes. Why didn't she reach out? Why didn't she say? We would have supported.

Marie was always so secretive. I guess she was ashamed of many things that had happened in her life. For whatever reason, she couldn't reach out and just wallowed in vodka. It was, and still is, heartbreaking. We found evidence that Marie was beginning to sort her life out, too. She had enrolled on some training courses and it looked like she was trying to sort her life out. There were training materials, notes and next steps. Back then, I never understood why she had died. I felt the most enormous guilt for not having spoken to her. Now, I was never going to speak to her in this world again.

I was tortured.

I couldn't get the thought out of my mind that she would never know how much I loved her and how special she was. In those moments, when life gives me a jolt, I remember the most random things; today was no different. A memory from childhood came flooding back: it was the day I had pushed Marie off the couch and she had broken her arm.

We were young children, maybe about five and seven years old respectively. Marie was the middle of three and I was the youngest. We grew up having a love/hate relationship. We would be best friends and worst enemies in the same minutes! This day was one of those days. Marie was sitting on the arm of the couch and I was on the seat next to her. I asked her to move, she wouldn't. I asked again, and, still, she wouldn't move. I kept repeatedly asking her! I did no more than push her from the arm of the couch. She fell with a bang and quite clearly was in a lot of pain. I remember lying to my parents and saying I hadn't pushed her, she claimed I had — she was telling the truth.

The same guilt that hit me when she died had hit me then, a slightly lesser degree when I was five but it was guilt all the same.

Marie died in Italy and her body needed transporting back to the UK. About 48 hours before her body was due to be repatriated, we received a phone call from the international funeral director. Marie had a small amount of cash, a ruby ring (grandma's) and her passport. The nature of transport in the cargo hold of a plane meant these items were likely to go missing in transit. A family member had to collect the items. Mum, Dad and Michelle did not have passports and as I was the only one with a valid passport, I had to do the deed.

Iain offered to come with me, but I thought it silly to waste two air fares. A couple of days after receiving the phone call requesting the personal collection of belongings, I got up at 3am and drove to Heathrow Airport. I could collect a flight at 7am and return at 5pm the same day.

I remember being very stoic: it was only a plane journey, no big deal, just flying to Italy and back in the same day, no biggie at all. How wrong I was!

The arrangement was to meet the funeral director on landing in the lower departures of Marco Polo Airport, Venice. My plane touched down on time and I texted the funeral director to say I'd landed. It was about 10.30 in the morning. We corresponded by text until we met in the departures drop-off area. The funeral director handed me Marie's passport, about £300 and Grandma's ruby ring. That was that. The sum of Marie's existence on holiday in my hands.

I still, to this day, have no idea what happened to Marie's clothes. It was about five hours before my return flight. There I was, alone with my thoughts, holding my dead sister's passport and looking at that picture knowing I would never see her again. I lit a cigarette and wept.

I cried like a baby, sitting on a seat outside Marco Polo airport.

This trip was much harder than I had expected. I posted on social media looking for support. I also calculated I could have two beers before needing to stop (I needed to drive again at Heathrow at the other end). I truly wanted to get drunk and forget where I was and why I was there. I cried and cried until there were no more tears left. I had the two beers and chain-smoked the entire five hours until it was time to get back on the plane. Landing back in London at about 9.30pm local time, I found the car and drove to Michelle's house. She was waiting there with the biggest hug.

I burst into tears in her arms. We wept together.

Marie's funeral arrived and Marie's son, Charlie, wanted to carry his mum's coffin. Iain was the only person of similar height in the family so was the opposite pall bearer to Charlie. West Bridgford Baptist Church was the venue for a celebration of Marie's life after a cremation. Michelle read the most beautiful eulogy, recognising the difficulties of Marie's life, but shared some of the most amazingly positive things Marie achieved in her life. Mum wanted to cater for the wake after the funeral. After much consternation, we all agreed but only on the understanding that she would leave instructions on the day and not interfere in the kitchen.

The week before the funeral, I spent a painstaking amount of time extracting from Mum's brain the plan for the food and writing it on Excel spreadsheets for the kitchen volunteers on the day. I remember all of the kitchen ladies complimenting Mum on the instructions and me smiling in the background. The event went without a hitch and was such a good send off for a much-loved sister.

Saying goodbye is very hard when you haven't seen the body. I grappled with the fact I had not seen my sister for six months. I started back at work just after the funeral and threw myself into the tasks at hand. I felt incredibly guilty and fought with the thoughts that Marie did not know how much I loved her before she died. It plagued me to such an extent that by that December, I was starting to suffer mentally.

One Sunday, I was packing for a business trip and just couldn't remember what I should pack.

I was lost and did not know how to function mentally. I am not sure if you have been in that place but I just sat on the black leather couch, crying. I kept trying to call Iain, who was away, but no joy. Eventually, I got through to Iain, who helped me pack over the phone and get myself to the airport. Iain was clearly worried but I was determined and didn't want to let anyone down by not going on the trip.

My thoughts continued to be plagued by the fact I hadn't spoken to Marie for months — now I was never going to ever speak to her in this world again.

I was tortured...

———————————————

*I'm startled from my dream: bump, bump! My head is hitting the gurney at great force ... step, step, step, bump, bump, bump. It seemed like moments since we were setting off with the gurney. I woke up looked around and realised we had arrived at High Camp...*

———————————————

# End of chapter challenge

After reading this chapter, you may have been triggered to reflect and think about your own circumstances. I am still very sad that Marie didn't reach out to her family. I know that as a family, we would have supported her. Maybe it was shame or pride. Who knows what stopped her? What I can say for certain is that you can choose to change your circumstances. Reflect today and if any of the issues Marie had are affecting you, choose to change them. The first step is admitting there is a problem. Ring one of the organisations in the appendix and start to talk ... they will help you with the rest.

# Chapter 3
# Shaken World

*We arrived at High Camp! The 12 porters were working very hard, I just don't remember it. When we stopped, my eyes opened and they were all sitting there, sweat dripping from their foreheads. They looked spent! We were not even one-third of the journey down. I apologised and thanked the porters, probably not for the first time, I just don't remember. There was a luxurious long drop in this location. To prevent any further embarrassment to my wonderful porters, I said I would take the opportunity to use this. I was helped off the gurney by the guide and a couple of porters; I was unsteady. My whole centre of balance was off. Fortunately, it was just a few steps.*

*I had an awful headache and, boy, the sunrise was bright! I kept saying to myself as I entered the 'ladies', (I say ladies, there was no difference in any long drop) 'I must not fall down the long drop.' For those of you inexperienced with the long drop, it is exactly as it says: a hole in the ground with a very long drop — and that is the toilet. As a gent, this is not too much of a problem. As a lady, aiming in the hole is an art form whilst also avoiding putting your foot in the hole. In addition, any distance away from the hole and the legs and ankles can get a little wet! Success ... I had managed to aim right and not fallen in — a miracle in the circumstances! I headed back out to the gurney and the ranger from the station at High Camp was waiting to take my O2 stats.*

*I clambered back onto the gurney and dutifully held out my hand. As soon as the oximeter had settled, my heart was 104 and O2 was seventy percent. The ranger yelled at all the porters in Swahili — I've no idea what he said but the last time I saw people move that fast was when Mum went into hospital in 2011.*

---

## Just coming round when....

It was 9th November, 2011 and Mum hadn't been well for a few days. This wasn't unusual for her. Mum was always quite ill as we were growing up. She had a condition which meant that fluid would accumulate in her body and her natural processes wouldn't get rid of it. She would go for what is known as a lumbar puncture. This procedure was used to remove fluid from her spine. After each procedure she would be knocked out for a few days. Lumbar punctures were pretty regular, I think every three to six months.

My understanding of all of this is rudimentary and gained in childhood. What I know is at nine years old, Mum went into hospital to have a new pioneering surgery: a shunt in the lower back. It would be normal for this condition to have a shunt fitted in the neck, but in Mum's case this wasn't possible. The pioneering back shunt was the only option. Being pioneering surgery, it would have its risks.

The procedure worked, and around about the August or September time of my tenth year, Mum came home from hospital. She was still poorly but on the mend.

Initially, the fluid was not being retained in her body; the valve worked, for a little while anyway. Then it went wrong.

Mum became violently ill and I will never forget returning home on my tenth birthday: I was so excited to walk in the door as I had received roller skates as a present. You may remember the type, those retro red roller skates that would be laced over your shoes. The metal could expand as your feet grew. You can imagine my excitement on the way home from school.

I walked through the front door to be greeted by a scene that I can only describe as horrific. Mum was violently throwing up on the couch. Apparently, something called her blood pressure (I was ten and didn't understand) was through the roof — whatever that meant. She looked as white as a sheet and was obviously in absolute agony. It pains me to remember it; in fact, writing this, I'm crying at the scene that I'm picturing. She was lying on our orange couch. I wasn't sure whether she would survive. The doctor attending my Mum was brilliant and as soon as the ambulance arrived, people were moving swiftly, but methodically, to get Mum into the back.

Mum had another shunt fitted. After three or four weeks stay in hospital, she came home and recovered. But the shunt failed again a few years later. Mum had an autoimmune disorder, which meant her body attacked itself, and she battled with that at the same time. She continued to be ill until she was diagnosed with a kidney fusing to her bowel. After her kidney was removed, some time later she had a heart attack.

During these few years, Mum went to the intensive care unit more times than I can remember.

In my A Level years, Mum sneezed and blew a hole in her head due to the fluid pressure in her head. Reader, this may sound so far-fetched but is true! Mum had a leak from her nose for three years and I remember being on an A Level biology field trip when Mum had surgery on her skull to repair the hole with bone from another part of her body.

Every time Mum went for a consultation, you would need a sack cart trolley for the notes and a shorthand typist whilst she was describing her history to whoever was treating her. Mum used to say that if you shook her up and down, she'd rattle due to the different medications she was on!

You may think that with all these illnesses, Mum would have been house and bed-bound but that could not be further from the truth. I could spend an entire book telling you the stories of Mum catering for weddings, making wedding dresses, crocheting baby's christening blankets, sewing absolutely anything from scratch, knitting pretty much anything and taking us on the most fantastic caravanning holidays.

Mum organised neighbourhood parties for bonfire night, catered when there was a power cut — such a talented and gifted lady. I could fill a book with funny stories about the caravanning holidays alone: the holiday where we spent a night on the A5; where we went ten minutes from our home in Nottingham via Scotland; the holiday where we ended eating ice cream for at least five days.

Remembering those moments now brings a smile to my face. So many great memories shared as a family because of Mum.

I am so proud and blessed to have had an amazing Mum.

Back to 9th November, 2011: Mum had become progressively ill over the week and the doctor came out. Mum was immediately shipped off to hospital in an ambulance, moving as quickly as those porters at High Camp! I arrived at the hospital that day and Mum was her usual stalwart self, thinking she would be out in days. She started telling me about the bread she needed to make and giving me instructions on how to make it.

Sadly, the infection Mum was fighting had moved and her bowel had stopped working. The surgical option of an operation was discussed but because of Mum's complex history, this was not a viable option. The surgeons feared that Mum would not have made it off the operating table. The only thing that was left was for Mum to fight the infection with the help of antibiotics.

The following day Mum, was drifting in and out of consciousness and getting increasingly confused with sepsis in her blood. I will never forget one conversation where Mum asked me, at the age of 37, whether I had been allowed out of school to visit her. She was clearly not well.

Mum had made it through times like this before with the many major surgeries. Why should this time be any different? We really didn't expect her to go and meet her maker. By the Friday, Mum was very poorly.

The consultants had decided to stop active treatment ... we agreed.

Michelle arrived and we sat with Dad for most of the Friday afternoon knowing that without a miracle, Mum was going to be with her maker soon. The doctors had removed all the active treatment lines and Mum was now in palliative care. I was so peaceful about the decision to no longer treat Mum, but I cannot describe the inner peace or where it had come from. It was the right decision, she had been in pain for so long.

This was just over two years after Marie had died. We had all started to get back to our lives. For me, grief didn't heal over time but life grew and continued to grow around it. I was at the point where hope and a future were beginning again; life was beginning again after Marie's death.

Now this. We were facing losing another.

Dad, Michelle, Charlie and I all sat with Mum. Dad was already quite poorly with a lung condition and was struggling in the hospital environment and heat. He needed to go home. We said 'goodbye' to Mum in case she passed into eternity. I drove Dad back home, then returned to the hospital.

Charlie went into one of the relatives' rooms for some sleep. Michelle and I sat there all night. We sang, read Psalms, held onto Bible promises and prayed with Mum. It was a really beautiful night, very peaceful. One of the nurses was amazing and just kept bringing us cups of tea. Michelle and I continued our vigil. It was the first time I had read a Bible in years.

I remember Mum saying something like 'oh dear, it's a right job this' at about 4am and then she never said another word. Michelle and I just smiled and could see she was peaceful. At around 6am, she was holding on and not going anywhere. I asked her to give me an indication that she wanted Dad back to hold her hand. I knew her hearing was still working, so I told her to let me know in some way. I felt the slightest twinge in her little finger. Dad and I arrived back to the hospital at about 8am. At 9:15am, Mum passed away into glory in the most peaceful way.

Mum's funeral was arranged soon after. Charlie, again, wanted to carry the coffin, so Iain dutifully stepped in for the second time and stood opposite him as pall bearer. When Mum arrived at the crematorium, we were expecting a few people. The place was packed! Mum would have been very happy! Following the committal, we held a celebration service at West Bridgford Baptist Church. Michelle spoke a fitting eulogy for Mum. And I wrote and read this poem:

## *An Ode to Mum*

*Here we are Mum to celebrate your life,*

*You were an amazing Mum and a brilliant wife.*

*We didn't expect your passing today,*

*But the angels decided they wanted your baking skills that way.*


*You left the flour in the mixer for the home-baked bread,*

*But St Peter decided he wanted you to bake homemade rolls for him instead.*

*In Childhood, At Christmas, Blackpool Illuminations on Westway we had,*

*Plus fun caravanning, bonfire nights, church camps and your mass catering weren't bad.*


*On our wedding days, your dresses made sure we were beautiful brides,*

*In knitting, sewing and dressmaking you were our ultimate guide.*

*Overall you were the most joyous fun,*

*Big hugs and kisses to you – we will miss you Mum xxx*

We did Mum proud with the catering and managed to feed half of Nottingham as well as the attendees at the funeral!

As I mentioned, Mum was very creative and very busy despite her illnesses. That resulted in a five-bedroom house full of stuff. One of the many things that brings a smile to my face is the stamps. Whenever the stamp price was being increased, Mum would go and buy books of stamps to save money. She was a thrifty sort. When she passed away, I opened Mum's stamp box and it was full. Michelle and I shared the contents between the two of us. Nine years later, my stamps ran out. Nine years of Christmas and birthday cards had been covered by Mum's stamps! And that was only half of them!

We scattered Mum's ashes on Christmas Day. Christmas Day was so important to Mum and Dad. It seemed an important thing to do together, the day that Christians celebrate Jesus's birth. There was never going to be a great day to do it, but this seemed right. We scattered the ashes on the Trent Embankment, with Dad in his wheelchair. He was struggling to walk anywhere by then due to the lung condition.

As we were scattering the ashes, the biggest gust of wind came along and blew them straight at Dad! It's the sort of thing that occurs in an average episode of Only Fools and Horses — it was very funny and I can imagine Mum would have been in hysterics at the very scene! Dad sneezed later in the day when he was in his rocking chair. Quick as a flash, he said, 'That's your mother,' causing much hilarity on what was quite a sombre Christmas Day.

After Mum died, we were floored! She had passed away seemingly quite suddenly. Dad was now alone in a big house and the black leather couch seemed like a great place to stay. I know I drank so much during that time. I remember drinking litres and litres of Jack Daniels and diet Coca-Cola. I cried and cried and cried. I spent a lot of time on that black leather couch. There was still a job to be done.

---

*Bump, Bump, Bump! Another set of steps. I open my eyes and reflect a little on the night I have just had. I had left camp early to stand the best chance of summiting Kilimanjaro at the same time as my teammates. Just to explain, I had been struggling with altitude throughout the climb. This night was no different. I had emerged from my tent at 8pm after a few hours of sleep. I was feeling so tired. I staggered to the mess tent to take on fluids and food before the summit attempt. I was not doing well and feeling rubbish. I had a headache and took one of the altitude sickness tablets.*

*I sat down and ate what I could from the bread put in front of me. When you read that altitude sickness causes a loss of appetite, I can confirm it does. My O2 was measured, and I was measuring at eighty percent, not excellent but sufficiently high to attempt the summit. My O2 saturation could not get any lower. As I was sat alone, Ben, one of the other climbers, came to pray with me. I was so grateful for that prayer. It felt like I was clinging onto God for dear life by this point.*

*It was dark and cold. The porter, the guide and I set off. I don't remember much of the journey out of camp; the terrain was wet and snowy and rocky. I was hanging onto the porter and the guide. I was struggling to step forward, my breathing was heavy, I was exhausted and that headache just wouldn't go! We continued upward. At around about 4,850 metres, was a moment I'll never forget: there was a rock covered with ice and I was holding onto both guide and porter but I slipped and fell over. I sat down and felt ill — the world was swaying, my breathing was heavy and I was struggling, shallow in shallow out. I could hear myself breathing ... I was straining. Everything was going into slow motion.*

*The guide ripped off my glove and put the oximeter on to take my O2 readings. It flashed up 'sixty-five percent' and my heart rate was through the roof. I remember it being high in the hundreds but don't remember the actual reading. My breathing was heavy. I was struggling even when seated. The guide looked at me, I don't think I will ever forget his words: "Sheralyn, the mountain will always be here; you will not if we continue." I think when someone tells you that your life is in the balance, you tend not to argue. I remember in that moment thinking 'I want my Mum' and remember crying. I was struggling to breathe as we descended back to camp.*

*When we arrived, the rest of our party was about to get the summit attempt underway. I was able to catch them in the mess tent. I walked into the tent and there was T Bone and Tim. T Bone gave me the biggest hug. I shared with him that I had the picture of my sister that I was taking up the mountain with me.*

*I asked him if he wouldn't mind carrying the picture to the top and capturing the moment. T Bone agreed and put it inside his favourite chapter of his book, 'Grounded and Cured' — his own story of fighting cancer. Taking Marie's picture up to the top of the mountain for me absolutely meant the world. The rest of the party left for their summit attempt. I was still struggling to breathe. It made me wonder if this was what it was like for Dad in his final months.*

---

## Breathless

Dad was diagnosed with COPD — chronic obstructive pulmonary disease — in about 2005. He had been both a miner and a heavy high tar smoker for about 40 years. He had stopped smoking six years earlier, but the damage to his lungs had been done. Initially, Dad carried on as normal with little effect, but over the years he had increasingly struggled to breathe. He used to sit in his armchair and say, 'I can change the world sat in the armchair but just as soon as I get up, I can't breathe.'

His health had seriously deteriorated since Marie died. By then, I had changed career to study law. When I did this, I asked Dad to promise that he would live to my graduation. He replied, 'I'll try my best ducky!' By the time Mum had died, Dad had been reliant on Mum for full-time care. He couldn't walk across the lounge without having to stop and take a rest.

He could hardly make the stairs and needed help dressing, showering and eating. He was so frustrated as, mentally, he could do anything — physically, he was falling apart. When Mum died, we were shocked as we always thought Dad would go first. His health had been deteriorating that badly.

## King Canute speaking

The days had long passed from his previous working life. Dad was works and transport manager for the local council. When there was local flooding and the council drainage system was blocked, our telephone at home was like a hotline. He would sit next to the telephone and answer the phone constantly, we had to stay out the kitchen and make no noise. It was rare to have a landline, but Dad needed one for work.

Dad would, after an hour or two answer, stating 'King Canute speaking'. At the time, I didn't understand who Canute was. I had no idea why Canute was an excellent response for Dad and amusing to all who heard it. I later learnt that Canute was quite an organised ruler and problem solver, just like my Dad. The only difference was, Dad was organising resources to solve the flooding and blocked drains in a local council rather than a whole country. Dad's work kept us in clothing, food and allowed us to have family holidays in Skegness. He was such a good role model of hard work. An amazingly loving Dad, we were blessed to have such loving parents.

## Supporting Dad

The tables had turned after Mum died and Dad needed intensive support. Michelle and I team-tagged with Dad: one staying at the family home each week each whilst also sorting out the many items Mum had accumulated. We would each prepare meals for Dad to freeze and eat on the odd days we were not there. After four weeks, it was clear we needed support. Social services said they would assess his case over six weeks and then would work out a care package — the six-week assessment was never completed.

Three weeks into the assessment, Christmas Day arrived. We prepared a meal at Dad's house, served after attending church. We knew this would probably be the final Christmas with Dad, so made the extra special effort. It was also the first Christmas without Mum. It was lovely to be at Mum and Dad's church with Dad. After scattering Mum's ashes, we went back to their house. We cooked Dad's favourite: beef. After dinner, we had some family game time, which was Monopoly around the table. It was so very special. It had only been about six weeks since Mum had died, so the memories were still very raw.

On New Year's Eve, Dad came over to my home for a meal. It was clear he wasn't ever going to stay awake to see the New Year in at midnight. With Mum gone, I don't think he was particularly interested in doing so either. By then, we regularly spent evenings with Dad at my parents' house. He used to look up at the ceiling on an evening and say, 'Hold the door open love, I'm on my way up!'

Dad left our house at 9pm on New Year's Eve and went home — 2012 was here...

On 2nd January, 2012, I received a phone call from the social services carer. Dad was struggling to breathe and was to be admitted to hospital by ambulance. I met him in accident and emergency and it was quite clear he was struggling. The hospital put him on a ventilation machine. He improved enough for a normal ward for a few hours but was very quickly transferred to the high dependency unit.

Eight weeks earlier, we had been there with Mum.

Dad was placed in the men's bay. I realised very quickly that his bed was the opposite side of the wall to where Mum had passed away. Dad was head-to-head, just the other side of the wall.

For the first few days, the nurses were different to those that nursed Mum. Inevitably, a nurse came on duty who had looked after Mum eight weeks earlier. When she saw us, she came over (after checking with us about whether Dad would be bothered) and Dad recognised her.

He turned to me and said, 'Oh, am I on the same ward as your Mum?' I replied, 'Yes, does that bother you?' He replied, 'Nah! I know I am in good hands.' And that was that — Dad's amazing pragmatism. I was reassured, as it could have had a traumatic impact, but it did not. The same stoic Dad! He continued that week living and surviving on the ventilation machine.

## Name, rank and number

Whilst in hospital, Dad and I reminisced about the 'work' we had to do for our 20p pocket money on Saturday mornings. We would line up in front of Dad in the order of our birth. Michelle would go first, Marie would be next and I would go last.

Dad would ask our name; I would say, Sheralyn. He would ask my rank; I would say youngest. Then, Dad would ask my number; I would say number three.

Dad would then ask us for the definitions of dexterity and ergonomics. We would have to reel this exact wording off (yes reader, I am not kidding, the EXACT sentences below) from about the age of 5 in my case. It took some remembering whilst writing this book!

- Dexterity — the manipulative ability achieved through good motor and perceptual coordination; and

- Ergonomics — the study of the relationship between the worker and the environment in which he works. In particular, the anatomical, physiological and psychological factors arising therefrom.

If, and only if, we recited these correctly did we get our 20p. This lesson was two-fold: Firstly, it amused Dad to have a five-year-old reciting these definitions, I think. Secondly, it taught us from a very early age that we had to work for our pocket money.

Years later, I was extremely thankful for reciting those definitions. I was in a health and safety exam and I had to answer the question, 'What is ergonomics?'

Dad was the first person I phoned on leaving the exam to tell him the good news. All his weeks of making us recite those definitions had proved practically useful to me in some way.

He was overjoyed then and still was now reminiscing in the hospital bed.

## Complications

A legal complication with Dad passing away too soon was that he was executor to Mum's estate. We had visited the solicitors the week after Mum died and signed executorship over to me, but we had not received word from the probate office that it was official. Every few days, I would need Dad to stay alive to sign things. On Saturday 7th January, 2012, the final notification from the probate office arrived. I received the notification before I went to visit Dad in hospital. That afternoon, two significant things happened...

Firstly, Michelle and I had invested in a small bottle of dad's favourite tipple: a blended whisky. It didn't look like Dad was going to come out of hospital, so what harm would a wee dram do? During the afternoon visit, I asked Dad if he wanted some whisky. He had been off the machine for about two hours and was feeling good.

When someone is in high dependency medical care, it is worth noting not to give them a normal measure of their favourite tipple — I speak from experience. Dad, on drinking the 'tea' I had prepared suddenly had all the alarms on every machine going off, his blood pressure when through the roof!

He started to laugh and then started to breathe heavily. His heart rate and the whole monitoring machine went berserk whilst nurses ran round him panicking and sorting things. He kept looking at me with his cheeky glint and pointed at me suggesting it was my fault, with a wink in his eye!

His face reminded me of the story he used to tell us about his friend, Digger Grant. His friend had bought us some life-size teddy bears one Christmas when we were children. When Dad went to collect them, Digger provided a whisky or two. Dad left Digger's house with the bears in each seat of the car. Dad was driving home when he was stopped by the police. The police officer did not know whether to laugh or breathalyse Dad when he saw the 'passengers'. Fortunately, he laughed and let Dad go on his way.

Secondly, Dad asked me if the probate office notification had come through. If I'm honest, I knew he was holding on for it; he had asked me every day when I was there if it had. I wasn't going to tell him the notification had arrived as I wanted him to stay alive. I also couldn't lie to him. I indicated it had, he sighed the biggest sigh of relief knowing he wasn't going to leave a small legal mess. It was then I knew it wasn't going to be long.

The following morning, 8th January, 2012, we received the call to attend the hospital and not worry about visiting hours. We knew it was time.

Dad had a poor night and was struggling. Michelle and I went to hospital.

As soon as we arrived, the consultant came immediately and confirmed what we all knew: the treatment wasn't working. Dad could not live on the machine forever. He had mental capacity and was part of the conversation, saying as clear as bell, 'Don't give a bugger what you do, make it quick, I know where I am going.'

At that moment, where he was looking at death, he was so faithful. He knew he was going to heaven. He could not wait to get there — to a place of no more suffering and pain. A place where he could breathe well again at last. Palliative care began about 10am and then at 2pm, he got his wish and went to join Mum. I won't forget Michelle turning to me in that moment and holding my hand, saying, 'Do not underestimate the impact of how losing three members of your immediate family in as many years will have on you!' She was right.

This was one of the most significant moments in my life. It changed my life in lots of ways. Don't get me wrong, the deaths of Mum and Marie had changed my life but Dad's death had let me see Jesus face to face. Dad's faith made me think twice about my own. How could he be so sure? How could he know?

His death was really beautiful in lots of ways. He was head-to-head with Mum on the same wall, but the other side. It was peaceful. I remember saying to him when he was under sedation that he had the best of both worlds: two girls holding his hand on the way out and two girls welcoming him at the other side.

Dad's funeral was a couple of weeks later. Michelle and I decided that it wasn't going to be as busy as Mum's funeral, so we catered for 30 fewer people. Well, quite the opposite was true! Before the service began, the minister stood up and asked everyone with a spare chair to put their hand up as it was standing room only. About 300 people attended Mum's funeral, about 400 attended Dad's. Michelle delivered an amazing eulogy again and I wrote another poem...

## *An Ode to Dad*

*So Dad it was time for you to join Mum and Marie and hold their hands,*

*A little sooner than we expected or indeed we had planned.*

*It is great you are together in God's wonderful house,*

*We hope you can enjoy a tipple of Bells, Grants or even Famous Grouse.*


*We had a wonderful childhood which we were able to reminisce and share with you,*

*A favourite memory of which had us in a queue.*

*Michelle ranked 1st and number 1, Marie ranked 2nd and number 2.*

*I was ranked 3rd and number 3,*

*Next, we had to recite the meaning of the words ergonomics and dexterity.*


*Our life lessons began with that Saturday pocket money 20p reward,*

*You nurtured supported and along with Mom made sure we were polite, hardworking, and never bored.*

*When life tripped us up and threw its curved ball,*

*You brushed us down cheered us up and taught us to carry on with God's call.*

*In our struggles at College, University and our working life,*

*You were there with a supportive word, a hug or just some good common-sense advice.*

*If a rocky road was then to be had,*

*One of the first phone calls was to good old Dad.*

*It was during one of these times when the blessing of Dad was near,*

*'What is ergonomics?' In the health and safety exam - the answer was clear.*

*And yes you guessed as soon as we were done,*

*Came a familiar phone call to Dad at home.*

*And so Dad in your own words we end this prose,*

*'Nanight, sweet repose, lie on yer back and yer not squash yer nose'*

*Good night Dad xxx*

The last line of that poem was what Dad used to say to us every night before we went to bed — if you hear me say this, it's continuing the tradition. I say it to lots of people now but especially Charlie at the end of every day.

After we said goodbye to Dad, we began the process of sorting out the house. And as I said, Mum was a hoarder. There were car loads of material for each school in the village. (They are probably still using stuff for school plays eleven years later!) There were three car loads of wool and knitting needles to Oxfam.

Mum used to have Tupperware parties, so there was cupboards and cupboards full of the stuff — this was all donated to church and, for weeks and weeks, the Tupperware was wheeled out to the mother and toddlers' group and sold on to raise funds.

My social media page looked like 'The Generation Game' with various items being offered free to a good home on collection. Memories on social media pop up occasionally and make me smile. The final social media status had to be a cuddly toy. In true Generation Game style, we took a picture of Michelle holding one of the massive Digger Grant teddies and offering it to a good home — it found one.

We saved Dad's ashes and decided we would spread them on Easter Day as that was the other significant day for Mum and Dad. The day when Christians celebrate the resurrection of Jesus. We stood at the same corner of the embankment: Michelle and her husband, Charlie, Iain and I... This time, no blowback and just a reverent goodbye to our parents.

# End of Chapter Challenge

Within the space of three years, my life had been turned upside down. These have been tough chapters to share. It really has. I am sure many of you will relate to the sorrow of it. What I would like you to do now, though, is remember the funny times and reminisce. When you went through those most traumatic moments in your life are you able to think of something happy or uplifting from those same moments? Ecclesiastes 3 says, 'There is a time for everything.' I'm going to leave you to go and find that and read it. I spent hours after this sitting reflecting on Ecclesiastes 3 on that black leather couch. Sadly, this lamenting was also accompanied by cigarettes and Jack Daniels with Diet Coke.

# Chapter 4
# Faith and the Couch Collide

*The rest of the group had left to attempt the summit. I was alone in camp and back at my tent. I shared earlier how low my O2 saturation was. This didn't improve throughout the night. Once I was back at camp, unless I was unconscious, it was clear I wasn't going anywhere quickly and would need to rest and wait for daylight. O2 at sixty-three is dangerously low. I am told that at that level, permanent organ damage can occur and even brain damage. At the time, I thankfully was totally oblivious to this information. That night, it may have made me panic; as it was, I knew I had altitude sickness, I had no clue as to the severity. It clearly wasn't severe enough to ship me off the mountain in the dark so that was cool by me. I went to sleep. My guide checked my O2 regularly with no change. I believe that coming through that night was nothing short of miraculous.*

*I was exhausted, so after the tears had flowed, rest was not difficult. Back in the UK, I later found out that someone was praying. Now for those of you not familiar with the acceptance of Jesus into your heart, what comes along with it are the most amazing family. People who care and pray in faith and 'know' without actually seeing for fact that their prayers are answered. In this case, a friend woke up at about 2am 'bolt upright' and felt the urge to pray for me. She started to do so in earnest but didn't know why she was praying, she just felt she needed to.*

*Early in the morning, she texted the rest of my close friends from our life group at church and asked them to pray as well. They all began praying. My O2 being that low could have caused a lot of permanent damage to my health or even caused me to meet my maker. But not this night. I believe that waking up the next morning was an answer to prayer. I was very thankful when I knew what had happened back in the UK that night, I had asked Jesus into my heart almost exactly seven years before.*

---

## New Beginnings Along With Sad Endings

After Dad passed away, I couldn't stop thinking about the circumstances of how he left this earth and how peaceful he was about it. I wanted that peace! I needed that peace — I needed to find it fast.

I made some enquiries and discovered a lively church, New Life Church, Derby (happy clappy as my Mum would say) in a deprived area of Derby. I went to church one Sunday evening, just after my birthday. I sat at the back of the church and began listening to the singing. I was totally overcome with emotion, I just cried the entire service. That first visit, I remember thinking my mum and dad were standing behind each shoulder with their hands on me, comforting me.

It felt like I was home.

I spent the next three weeks crying as soon as worship started. It was like something was touching me and getting to the root of my grief.

So hard to describe but being in the church gave me a sense of being wrapped in a comfort blanket when grieving for my parents.

I kept returning to church week after week. I was looking for something and I thought I might find it here. There was a massive hole in my heart. Something was missing. I was hurting. I needed something or someone to help me.

I invited Iain but he did not want to join in on my newfound journey — I know at the time, he thought I was being introduced to a cult. (New Life Church is far from that, just for those who do not know the church.) I continued to go to church week after week. Halfway through the year, I was invited to join an Alpha Course. I had heard of the course before but had never attended. I signed up and asked Iain whether he wanted to join me. Begrudgingly, he agreed.

We both attended the first couple of weeks on the course but after week two, Iain said he didn't believe in God and did not want to return. I wasn't going to force him. It really was his personal choice. I continued to go to Alpha and learned more about the Christian faith, dispelling the myths about how hard I needed to work to connect with Jesus. Connecting with Jesus was as easy as praying a prayer, He would then be in my life.

Grief was overtaking my existence. My weekly drinking was getting out of hand with me drinking two litres of Jack Daniels, plus wine on top. I needed something else, something healthier than alcohol to turn to and be comforted by. 'Alpha Day' arrived on 10th November, 2012 — it was a year since Mum had died.

'Alpha Day' is often referred to during the course. The only way I can describe it, if you haven't tangibly felt Jesus up until this point, is that you feel Jesus on that day (if you want to that is). You see, we are given free choice. If you don't want to believe, then you don't have to. What successive Alpha teams find is that many people feel Jesus's presence for the first time on that day. Healing takes place and miracles happen. This was definitely the case for me. I felt that the hole in my heart was being filled, that I had found something that could help comfort me at my time of grief. I prayed the simple prayer to ask Jesus into my heart. I suddenly felt light and hope again. I felt peace.

Many people will tell you all the good things about having Jesus in your heart. There are so many and you will see this throughout the rest of the book. But a word of warning, don't believe that life just becomes plain sailing when you accept Jesus into your life...it doesn't. The storms still come but the difference is, Jesus is there to help you steady the boat through those storms.

As you can imagine, the deaths of Mum and Dad within the space of eight weeks was catastrophic to our whole family. I had to defer my law studies for a year. In September 2012, I continued my Graduate Diploma in Law. I completed the course with a commendation and graduated in 2013. Dad was not there to see me graduate. The day was filled with a tinge of sadness that he was not there to join me. I know Mum and Dad would have been very proud.

Following my graduation, I studied the Legal Practice Course full-time. I threw myself wholeheartedly into my studies, starting at 6am and then sitting in the library until 8pm most nights. I was rewarded for my hard work with a distinction on the Legal Practice Course. During that year, I had a mentorship with a law firm, completed training contract applications with many law firms and attended interviews...all to no avail! I was not successful at getting the elusive training contract I needed.

I was throwing everything at a possible legal career as a solicitor. There is a Bible passage that says when God opens a door, no man can shut it and when God closes a door, no man can open it. The qualification road to being a solicitor seemed well and truly shut. On reflection, it was clear that I was spending all my time and attention on law and neglecting things at home.

I failed to see the coming storm.

I completed my Legal Practice Course in July and was looking forward to the summer relaxing with Iain. I went on a two-week international law school, leaving Iain at home. On my return, we went on holiday.

Things seemed quite strange between us, but I couldn't figure out why. We went to sports events and explored cities, but our relationship was strained. In October 2014, it was clear something was wrong, and I received the devastating news that Iain was not happy with our relationship. Iain came home from work one day and said he had something to tell me. He took me and sat me on the black leather couch and revealed how he felt about things.

I immediately reflected at the last year and realised the strain my studies had put on our marriage after such a period of trauma in my family.

My world crashed completely at the thought my marriage was ending too.

This feeling was very different, completely different to anything I had experienced previously. I was overcome with grief again: the thought that I might lose the man who had carried the coffins of my sister and parents, and that he no longer loved me. I made a decision on that black leather couch that day, a decision that would take me through another agonising and all-consuming eight months. A decision that I wanted to save my marriage. I only needed Iain to want to save it too.

When I accepted Jesus into my life in 2012, I knew he had forgiven me all my sins I, therefore, had to forgive anyone else. It hurt when Iain told me the truth but the Bible tells us we all fall short of God's glory. Iain was no different and I had to forgive and try and rebuild. We both agreed on that black leather couch to continue working on our relationship. Neither of us were willing to give up on our nineteen-year relationship at that point. We had been through so much and I'd lost a good proportion of my immediate family; I really didn't want to lose him too.

We crawled through to Christmas with stresses and strains. Whilst I was trying to behave in a normal way, Iain looked so guilty every time he looked at me. I asked him many times about it, he was racked with guilt at how much he had hurt me. I kept trying to tell him there was an amazing antidote to his feelings if he would entertain looking in the same direction that I had — towards Jesus. Iain did not want to know. It caused a lot of tension and I have no idea how we hid the strain in our relationship from his mum, who had come to stay with us over Christmas.

The New Year arrived and we travelled to Amsterdam to see the New Year in. Iain was not himself: his mood and melancholy made the trip extremely strained. When we returned home, the atmosphere between us was bad. As hard as I tried to continue life as normal, Iain seemed to sink deeper and deeper into depression. It came to a head at the end of January. He left me. I was devastated. I was panicked. I was floored. I prayed.

Michelle came straight to see me and stayed with me. I recognised the feelings of grief. Grief was no stranger, not only was I torn apart by the grief of it, but the big questions also came: how was I going to pay the mortgage? How was I going to pay the bills? I had not yet retained a full-time job in law, I was only working a few days as a paralegal. Fortunately (and at the time I know it was a real God send), I was in a matrimonial law firm, so had some great advice without it costing me a second mortgage.

Approximately a week after Iain left, he contacted me and said he had made a big mistake and wanted to return and try again. Jesus died for my sins, I needed to forgive Iain and try again. I was keen to give our marriage another try but wanted to do so wisely. After chatting with the solicitors, I set out the terms of an agreement in which Iain could return home and we could work on our marriage. He agreed to the terms and over the next few weeks completed all the practical steps needed.

These steps ensured that, should Iain decide he wanted to leave again, I had financial security and could stabilise until I found full-time employment. Iain moved back in at the end of February.

We agreed to counselling and turned to a very well-known marriage counselling organisation. I am not aware of anyone else's experiences with this organisation, but, for us, it felt like 'a cup of tea and sympathy' counselling. The lady appeared to be a well-meaning volunteer who was not qualified in counselling techniques. We needed someone to take our marriage apart as individuals.

The 'counsellor' was intent on taking us through a process rather than looking at us as individuals and tailoring the approach. Very quickly we both became despondent with the process and didn't want to go to the sessions. It became clear towards the end of April that Iain was still battling with one or two things.

I suggested to Iain that the counselling we had received before was not 'proper' counselling. We needed to find a qualified professional to help us. He agreed. We engaged a private couples' counsellor who was brilliant. Within 30 minutes of listening to us, he had identified and pinpointed problems in our relationship. The counsellor was very good at making sure we both had a say. He drew Iain into talking freely in a way I had never seen before. I'm not sure he always got a good opportunity in the talking stakes mind with me as his wife!

We both seemed to like going to the counselling sessions and we were starting to see what needed healing in our marriage and what needed to happen next.

We continued to see the counsellor and had a great session at the end of May. Iain had spoken more freely than ever before in that session.

You can imagine my surprise (and the surprise of the counsellor) when three days later, Iain said he wanted to finally walk out on our marriage. I was so angry and when we returned home, immediately emptied all his clothes from the wardrobes onto the black leather couch then slumped down on top of them and cried. I cried and cried. I was so angry. I kept asking God 'why?' in prayer and asking Him to change it. There was no changing it, Iain had decided and that was that. I was devastated...again.

It would be very easy to sit here and write this account blaming Iain and I hope you feel I have not done that. He is a good man. We both made mistakes in our marriage — it does 'take two to tango' as the saying goes. I had not done my part of the tango any more than Iain...it took a few years for me to realise that. I believe that when I had accepted my part in the failure of the relationship, I was able to truly heal.

---

*I awake and open my eyes. It's a while since we left High Camp. I do not know what woke me or how long we had been journeying down the mountain. I had absolutely no concept of time. I just kept closing my eyes and wishing we were down at the bottom of the mountain.*

*It may have been the fact that I was vertical that awoke me from my reflections. I opened my eyes and all I could see were tops of trees.*

*I looked down and immediately felt sick — it was a long way down and the porters were clearly manoeuvring behind me with the gurney.*

*Oh my goodness! I was praying.*

*I was frightened. I couldn't see anyone and felt I was just being jolted in every direction. I was, by this time, feeling so low. I had failed the summit. I had failed in my challenge! I had to tell the world who had been supporting me that I was failure, that is if I lived through this experience. I was overwhelmed. I was alone. Almost my lowest point in my life.*

---

## Stuck on the Couch

The lowest point of my life in memory was 3rd June, 2015. I am bereft...I have come from the bed to the black leather couch and am wallowing in grief and pity. I have put on my 'go to' films. First I watch 'A Few Good Men': a story of injustice. This is just what I feel right now. I get to the scene where Jack Nicholson screams 'you can't handle the truth' to Tom Cruise. Jack Nicholson is right! The tears just keep flowing. I reach out for the glass of red wine from the bottle I have just opened. Plenty of time to be too drunk to face the next day. I swig! There is a full bottle of Jack D in the cabinet, I have at least 20 cigarettes and I am wallowing, wallowing, wallowing...

My life was over as I knew it: I'd lost my sister; I'd lost my parents; I'd lost my marriage. I had a big glass of wine in my hand and that black leather couch was enveloping me. I felt like I was losing the little faith I had gained. Where was God in this? He hates divorce! I was about to embark on just that. Did he hate me, too? I was watching Lord of the Rings (extended edition) for the umpteenth time and had a cigarette in my hand, the third in succession. The tears kept coming. I felt bereft and depressed. My world had come crashing down.

I kept thinking about Iain carrying the coffins of my family. I cried and cried!

I want Mum and Dad more than I had ever wanted them before, and they were not there.

What was the point of it all? I was wallowing in self-pity. I was slumped on the black leather couch from Wednesday through to Sunday — smoking, crying, drinking, smoking, crying, drinking. No one would have known at the time that this was what I was going through; I think I hid it well.

From that week on, I would go to church on a Sunday and sing in the choir — looking like the life and soul of the party on stage and praising Jesus. The happy nature of church meant I could be my outgoing self and jump around and pretend life was great and smile and chat with one and all. Please, reader, do not misinterpret this: the Bible tells us to praise the Lord in all circumstances and I was. I could do little else.

Only that wasn't the whole picture!

Inside, I was far from praising the Lord. I would maintain this happy external persona until after the Tuesday choir rehearsal. Again, smiley, happy and the life and soul of the party, I'd return home on Tuesday night and slump onto the black leather couch and begin to drink and drink into the small hours, maybe watching 'Star Wars', 'In the Name of the Father', 'A Few Good Men', 'Lord of the Rings'... The phrase 'tears of a clown' spring to mind! I would be happy from Sunday to Tuesday and then back onto the black leather couch for the rest of the week.

I grappled so much with my faith here. In Christian circles, it is easy not to recognise when people are going through very real pain. It can be labelled 'spiritual attack'. We are told the enemy is having a go — of course he is, but we also suffer from the same human emotions as the next person! Ecclesiastes 3 says there is a time for everything.

As a group of God-fearing people, I am not convinced that we know quite how to deal with the 'everything' that Ecclesiastes refers to. It is easy for someone looking on to pray about spiritual attack and, by doing so, leave someone feeling condemned that they are still depressed. Storms in life will have an impact on our emotions and, yes, I do agree that Jesus is in the storm with us. That doesn't stop us having human feelings and depression and suicidal thoughts.

Being advised by well-meaning people who love Jesus that we need to 'praise in all circumstances' left me feeling that I could not be honest with anyone about what I was going through. I could not be honest about feeling that I wanted to end my life and I could not be honest and turn to the very people that could support me.

I felt alone, I was holding on to my faith as much as I could. I wanted to end the pain then I would remember my saviour carrying that pain on the Cross.

I remember sitting on the black leather couch thinking that I would end my life and the process of how I was going to do this. I wanted a method that was least impactful to anyone. Trains, cars and any other moving vehicles were out — what about the poor person(s) driving or travelling by that mode of transport. Slitting my wrists seemed extremely painful and messy. In addition, it would be quite hard to do both wrists and inflict that pain to make sure I had completed the task at a hand. I am a wuss with physical pain!

I'd pretty much decided that pills were the only way for me to end it. My biggest problem was knowing what concoction to use. For those people who don't know me, you would have to search high and low in my house to find a paracetamol or an ibuprofen. Finding enough pills of a strong enough quality was a massive problem. Thankfully, without good medical knowledge and research it is quite tough to take your own life.

There are many stories of people who have tried to take their life and failed, leaving catastrophic physical injuries instead — I didn't want that. There are also a distinct lack of websites, again, thankfully, that chart successful suicide attempts from pills. I am so very thankful that I did not have the knowledge or the understanding as to how and what method would be best to take my own life.

I don't think anyone around me at the time knew I was thinking these things. I wasn't sharing it, I was so ashamed. I was in pain.

I felt other people had worse traumas than I. There is no easy comparison for trauma. One person's trauma can seem like nothing to another's. Our trauma is based on our life experience, our skills and our ability to cope. Someone can lose a pair of glasses and it'd be very traumatic for them, usually because of some past trauma or consequence. There are people out there right now reading this book who are in that dark place of isolation. I want to say to you: YOU WERE BORN FOR A REASON; YOU ARE LOVED; YOU ARE VALUED; YOU ARE MADE FOR A SPECIAL PURPOSE.

During those dark days, I also discovered reading the Bible. I had asked Jesus into my heart but hadn't read the historic manuscript behind my decision. You probably won't be surprised to know that many people haven't read the Bible. If you are reading this and you haven't, please do so before you decide to neglect its teaching... but start with the New Testament! The Old Testament is there for a reason but can be heavy going to understand.

When I started reading the Bible, I began to follow a plan which started in the book of Job. For those who don't know this book, the central character, Job, loses his family, livelihood, home and health. His 'friends' condemn him saying he must have done something wrong to deserve that judgement. The reader quickly learns that it is not a loving Father God but Satan who has caused this. Job keeps praising, even though he doesn't understand. There is one point when he is full of self-pity but then a younger friend steps in. The end of the story sees Job restored and blessed twice as much as he was before.

It made me realise that there is always someone worse off than me. I needed to count the blessings I had: I still had a home and a cat and my lovely New Life Church family. I began to hold onto my faith in Jesus like I had never held on to anything before.

I remember, as a child, Mum and Dad had a poster by the front door. It was a kitten clinging onto the handle of a large wicker basket. The handle was huge and towered way above the basket, so the kitten was clinging in midair with a panicked look on its face, hanging on for dear life so as not to fall. Above the picture was the caption: "Faith isn't faith until it's all you're holding on to." I will never forget that poster.

And that was just how I felt now.

I was holding on for dear life to anything that would get me through. That was my faith in Jesus, my hope in Jesus, the peace that Jesus would bring. If you are reading this and you are just holding on, reach out to someone, anyone...reach out. I remember thinking I could not be honest, I could not reach out. I was ashamed, I was lonely, I thought I would be a burden. Let me assure you: YOU ARE NOT A BURDEN, YOU ARE LOVED, YOU ARE SPECIAL. REACH OUT TODAY.

# End of chapter challenge

The black leather couch in this story so far has seen lots of action, some negative and some positive. In the positive, it is a comfy place for cosy nights in and watching the TV. I am pretty sure the idea for this book came from that black leather couch. The couch, though, can be a place where you get stuck; where you get rooted; where it is so comfortable you don't want to move. It's so safe, you don't want to get up from it.

The challenge here is to be honest with yourself. That is quite difficult. It is very easy for us to sit and judge what others are doing and saying but difficult for us to judge ourselves. Look around you and ask those closest to you if you need to. Are you stuck on a couch? Do you go and take everything that life has to offer? Or do you put barriers in the way before you commit to things? Are you your own worst enemy when it comes to living life to the full? Do you project onto people your negative views and behaviour of yourself? Do you encourage others? Do you build them up? Are you the first to spot the positive or the negative in someone?

These are all questions you can ask yourself. If you are honest, you will work out which parts of your character are stopping you from getting somewhere and change them.

If you are in that place and you need support, feeling that you can't go on, here are some numbers of organisations that can help you....

Premier Lifeline – 0300 111 0101, https://www.premierlifeline.org.uk/who-we-are

Samaritans – 116123, https://www.samaritans.org/how-we-can-help/contact-samaritan/

MIND - https://www.mind.org.uk/need-urgent-help/

**SHERALYN PATTISON**

# Chapter 5
# It's in the Waiting

*Bump, bump, bump! At every step down, my head is banging forcefully on the back of the metal gurney. I am more aware than I was before of the gurney and its discomfort. I totally understand its design and I am quite thankful that they are taking me off the mountain quickly – though it's not so comfortable. My health is clearly improving as I am more aware of just about everything, the porters are working so hard. I can see the sweat dripping from their faces. There is a team of twelve. They alternate every so often. It is a matter of patience and waiting now to get to the bottom. Us human beings are not so good at waiting and patience though!*

---

## The Departure Lounge

January 2016 and a new chapter in my life must start. Enough wallowing! I sat in church and Kevin Shaw is preaching. It's an average Sunday and being honest, I can't say I have listened to many sermons whilst in church over the last six months. My mind has always been wandering. This Sunday, something Kevin said piqued my interest. He started talking about airports.

I had embarked on many a journey with Iain, and then a fair few without him, so I could relate. I reminisced during this sermon about how brave I thought I had been about ten years previously when I boarded a plane on my own to Europe and then the USA for work. I snapped back into consciousness when Kevin started talking about the different stages of check in: Check in at the desk (this was the days before online check in); passing through security; then waiting in the lounge; boarding call; final call; delayed; cancelled!

Kevin likened this to our walk with Jesus in our lives. When you first accept Jesus, you've just checked in and passed through security. All the excitement awaits, and you are on the way. Then comes the wait in the departure lounge, likened to different seasons of our life. Sometimes, the plane was on time and there was a little wait; sometimes the plane was slightly delayed and sometimes the plane didn't take off at all.

At this point, I felt the sermon was for me. Everyone has a choice about how they wait in the departure lounge. Do you go straight to the gate and sit there getting tetchy that you are not boarding and getting impatient? Do you go and busy yourself with something, such as reading a book, knitting, craftwork and just wait for the boarding call? Do you go shopping eating, drinking to pass the time whilst awaiting the call? I was certainly the latter of the groups and would socialise, eat and drink before my plane journey. Kevin went on to say that sometimes our plane gets delayed and we are forced to wait. It is what you do in the waiting that matters.

I had spent the last six months wallowing, so it was about time to stop. Time to do something more productive in the departure lounge.

For me, 2016 was a year of lingering in the waiting room, and a time of healing. A lot had happened in such a short space of time and I needed to process it. I would share my circumstances with people, and they would be incredulous as to how my life had become something akin to a Coronation Street script rather than an average existence. As an extrovert and someone who processes externally, I struggled being alone and trying to process. I began to live again and instead of waiting at the gate, I got busy in the airport lounge. I must be honest, not everything I got busy with was productive. I had quite the reputation of the happy party drunk. Much of my time was spent in company doing just that...partying.

Whether you were inside my church circles or outside, you would find me getting drunk and partying. In this period of my life, I did many things I was not proud of, which would not accord with my Christian faith and values. To an outsider, I would have looked like I was having fun. Inside, I was crying out for help, wracked with guilt about my behaviour and probably hurting more people around me than I would have wanted. If you are reading this and you are one of those people, I hope you can forgive me.

I was going to have to wait in that departure lounge for what God had on offer. But I needed to do something positive to stop this wallowing and melancholy — it was doing me no good at all.

My liver and kidneys were screaming too! Charlie had lost his mother and had a traumatic upbringing. I had been supporting him a lot since Marie died and, after five years, it felt right to open my home. He had many issues from childhood but I felt a steady home and some encouragement would help. He moved into my house in March 2016.

In April 2016, I also took my first holiday after the breakdown of my marriage. It was a cruise holiday around the Caribbean. I tried new things and met some wonderful new people. I am still in contact with some of those people — one day I will make it to see them again as they were such a lot of fun. I see those memories crop up on social media and they always make me smile.

This cruise represented a new me, a single me, one who had to begin the process of discovering my identity again. Those of you who are married or in long-term relationships will know that you become intertwined with one another. You begin to think what the other might say, how they may react in a situation and what they will agree to as well as decisions about dinner, what to wear, decorations in the house, the bills and pretty much everything are collaborative. When that partnership ends, you need to start making those decisions again, alone. Initially, that is a very scary process.

I bought a painting at my first-ever art auction on that cruise. I saw it from the back of the room and just stuck my hand up. As the maiden bidder, I purchased it successfully. The painting sits above my mantelpiece at home. From the back of the auction room, it looked like a bright orange sunset, I could not see it closely.

When I went to view the painting up close later, I burst into tears. It was beautiful! It was indeed a sunset. Two ships were sailing towards the sunset and a bright horizon. The ships' masts looked like the crosses on

Calvary. It was just perfect to represent that stage in my life and my faith.

On the cruise ship, I was musing about wanting a 'glamping' van, caravan or camper van. My car at the time wouldn't tow a caravan, so camper vans would be the best option. My friend found a converted long wheelbase Ford Transit up in Liverpool. We drove up to see it and I bought it. I had never made such a big purchase on my own. This was a giant step for me and for my independence. The camper van (Freda the Ford) represented my new-found freedom.

I spent so many weekends over the next two years attending festivals and living away in the van. I loved just pulling off the driveway and going! I became an expert reversing on and off the narrow driveway. I also have a very understanding neighbour who lost one or two plants from her garden along the way! When I wasn't travelling, I began volunteering at the local mission, Derby City Mission, doing whatever I could to help. I had the legal qualifications but did not know what to do with them. I kept turning up like a bad penny hoping one day they might employ me. I was part of a lively church community and began to throw myself wholeheartedly into it. Life began again in 2016. I was still waiting for the next moves though and it was really a year of waiting and healing.

---

*Thank goodness! The bump, bump, bump had temporarily stopped. I was still propped up and strapped into the gurney. We were somewhere in the rainforest area now. The landscape was teaming with natural wildlife — the birds were beautiful. The porters were taking a rest and eating something as they had worked so hard. I am sure if I had asked, they would have unstrapped me to let me exercise but it just didn't occur to me. As we were sitting there, over in the distance were some monkeys. They were watching our every move. I suspect they were waiting for the crumbs that were left once we set off again. It reminded me of home and I wondered how Dottie would be coping without me.*

---

## Dottie

It is well documented by psychologists that pets are great for human mental health. My mental health was not in a great place. Charlie was still living with me. Towards the middle of the year, I started looking at puppies and the possibility of getting a dog. I knew it would get me active. I had spent the last twenty years or so doing no exercise. I needed to get fit, and a dog would help me do this. A dog would also be a great incentive for getting Charlie active and socialising. I started looking at puppies and decided that it had to be a cockapoo. After researching the breed, I thought about taking two puppies from the same litter. The first litter I checked out were lovely but looked more like labradors. I searched again and found a breeder in Lincolnshire and spoke to him at length. He said the waiting list for puppies stretched to spring 2017.

I was prepared to wait and arranged a visit to check them out.

Visiting day arrived and it turned out he was important in the cockapoo world and interviewed me for three hours to check that I knew what I was taking on before he would let me look at a dog. He wanted me to understand that both parents were working dogs and would need plenty of exercise. He also checked that I understood about 'separation anxiety' as cockapoos commonly suffer. Once he was satisfied my situation would accommodate a cockapoo, I was introduced to all the girls and boys that they owned. I was allowed to pay my deposit for a puppy the following spring. I waited for the call to say a pup was available.

I had not worked for any employer for some time. My last job ended when I stepped away to study law full-time in September 2013. I considered applying for a job as a support worker with Derby City Mission at the night shelter towards the end of 2016. It was a less taxing role than my previous job as a UK-wide health and safety manager and I'd work just two nights a week. I had volunteered at the night shelter and other homeless projects since 2012. I was successful in getting the role and was looking forward to starting the four-month long role from December 2016.

About four weeks before the role started, I received the call to say that a puppy was going to be available in the next two weeks. I would have the puppy before my night shelter role began.

I knew this wouldn't be an issue as Charlie was at my house most of the time, so he could look after the pup when I was not there. He was excited to be part of the selection process.

I was invited to a selection evening and all six puppies from the litter were running round. One pup came and sat calmly on Charlie's knee and then with me. That was the one! I had to wait until the following day to find out if she was going to be coming home with us. It is commonly stated that dogs choose their owners and this one certainly did. I think it's the first time Charlie saw me pray for something. On the way home, we stopped at a restaurant and I audibly prayed for that puppy.

The following day, I was attending a first aid course. My concentration on that course wasn't the best: all I could think about was the telephone call from the breeder. At 3.30pm, a call came and there it was...success, the pup was ours. Charlie saw his first answer to prayer. Dottie joined us two weeks before my night shelter job started. My new family was developing. We would regularly sit on the black leather couch together!

---

*Bang, bang, bang! This gurney is starting the get painful on my head again — I must be feeling better. I sit up and start singing praise songs. I can do little else. I reflect and remember the last time I sung a praise song on the mountain. It was about twenty-four hours earlier as I awoke to begin the long day-five trek.*

*Life was very tough going for me on the mountain, I really struggled due to the O2 and lack of acclimatisation.*

*I trekked for longer, didn't need to be told 'pole, pole' (slowly in Swahili) as I was just plain old slow. Every day at 6am, I would sing a praise song and grace all with a tune. I know most people appreciated it, some did not. It was the only way I could carry on with the journey; to hand the situation to God and carry on.*

*On the gurney, I continued singing — we were getting somewhere. I was feeling so much better than I had in days. The problem with sitting up on the gurney was the poor chap at the front was taking my entire weight bearing down on him. I had totally missed the physics of the stretcher's design and us descending! My guide came and told me to lay down again. I was feeling physically better. I was healing.*

---

## Bright New Future

In 2017 my life began — it felt like a weight had lifted. Jesus had been close, and I could feel the healing coming. Don't get me wrong, I was still lonely at times but I started to feel like I was whole again. I am sat in church one Sunday. Henry Ita was preaching. He preached a word about fruitfulness in the church and the fruitfulness in families and businesses in the church. This sermon really spoke to me. I had been contemplating starting a business and my Master of Laws (LLM) supervisor had confirmed I had sufficient qualifications to start up a business performing non-reserved private client work in wills and probate.

I came away from church thinking about what the most important steps were to starting my legal business.

I needed to decide what to call it, find an indemnity insurer, develop a logo and open a bank account in the business name. I looked at company structures and decided a sole trader was right for this business.

The next day, I began in earnest. By the end of the day, Derby Legal Assistance was created with full logo, bank account and indemnity insurance, starting on 1st February. This was all a complete Godsend. Setting up a business normally takes a lot longer! In two weeks, I would be self-employed. I created a social media page and began advertising.

I hadn't quite realised how brave going from a standing start was in building a business. It always takes time for word to spread, and for people to come to you. I did quite quickly realise I needed another source of income for a few years. I applied for a couple of roles but came second behind the successful candidate each time. I needed to clear my head!

In summer, I took a three-week adventure in Freda, with Dottie by my side. I travelled to France. I had never driven all that way alone before — or on the wrong side of the road. I stayed near the ferry in Canterbury the night before we went. I drove onto the boat but Dottie had to stay in the van with the windows slightly open. The kind ferry staff found me a spot where I could see the van and see if Dottie was distressed. She settled on the seat and remained so the whole journey.

I drove off the ferry onto the autoroute and travelled straight to my first campsite. The toll booths in France were a bit of a pain as I was on the right-hand side of the vehicle. We reached the site in good time and I remember being stupidly proud of myself for getting this far. Travelling alone on a road trip was a liberating experience. I was very thankful to God for the lack of problems and felt completely at peace. The world would have you believe that it is not safe for a lone female to travel into a foreign country on their own: too dangerous, too vulnerable. I believe with God anything is possible. There is such a peace in your heart and soul when you know this. You know that no matter what happens, He will guide and sort it out.

I had an amazing time in France. I walked Dottie along rivers, up hills and around quaint French villages. The great thing about having a dog in France is dogs are welcome everywhere. There were only two places I found where she wasn't welcome, understandable on both counts: Notre Dame Cathedral and a champagne vineyard and tour. We had a great three-week adventure. I was starting to believe in myself again. I was starting to love myself again.

When my marriage broke down, I had started to question who I was and whether I was nice and likeable. I had become insecure and less confident. I listened at church every Sunday and knew in my head that Jesus loved me as I was. In my heart I was not accepting it. I was thinking: How could Jesus like a divorcee? How could anyone, in fact? Forgiveness is the key.

A long time since, I had forgiven Iain and reconciled that we would never be a couple again. What I had not done up until now was forgive myself.

I believe it takes two people to make a relationship and two people to break it. Our own behaviour can contribute to the final 'straw that breaks the camel's back'. I had not forgiven myself for my own behaviour. In France, I began to do this. What right did I have to hold unforgiveness to myself when Jesus had given his life to forgive all my sins? I didn't have any right at all — I needed to forgive myself and the true healing would come. This realisation really hit me in France when I was on my own, reliant on God to ensure my safety.

I returned from France and Charlie decided he did not want to stay with me any more, so moved back in with friends. I was alone again but this time I had a peace about being alone at home. I no longer detested driving onto the driveway, I loved getting into the house and relaxing on the black leather couch.

---

*Each step down now is just so present. My head is banging constantly on the gurney. It has been for a few hours, but each bump is more in my consciousness then ever. Suddenly, I feel a panic! How would Hope for Justice feel about my early exit from that mountain? The shame of not having summited hit me: I was a failure.*

*The mountain had defeated me.*

*People would judge me. And everyone would know about it.*

*I would never be able to face anyone in head office again. I continued to ponder as my head was banging almost relentlessly on the gurney. You may wonder why Hope for Justice...*

---

## Welcome to my World — Hope for Justice

Around July 2017, I was scrolling through social media on the black leather couch and saw a job advert for an Independent Modern Slavery Advocate It was a part-time role for a charity called Hope for Justice. The advert flashed up and I saved the link from the charity's website in my browser. I remember trying to find the advert on social media again and I couldn't. It really felt like this was God providing the perfect opportunity. I could still build the legal business and work for a charity that I could relate to.

I had first heard of the charity at a women's conference in Leeds in 2016. I immediately signed up to be a guardian and sent in my CV to volunteer. I heard nothing back. When I saw the job advertisement, I just knew this role was for me. I was nervous but had a confidence that I was about to leave the departure lounge and be called to board the plane. Ironically, Henry, my pastor, had asked me if I was interested in modern slavery in 2014. I had said it was not the area of law I was heading in. Here I was three years later applying to work directly with modern slavery survivors.

I applied and was invited for interview. I remember being stupidly excited to stand next to the 'Freedom Wall'. The Freedom Wall is a set of red padlocks with names and dates on. Each padlock represents a person rescued from slavery by Hope for Justice.

I produced a musical video of photographs for my interview as a presentation, drawing on my skills and abilities to perform in the role. I wanted to avoid a 'Death by PowerPoint' presentation, so I opted for a musical video. I prayed like I had never prayed before about any job. I was desperate for the role.

The role involved a lot of travel, but I was hungry for the job. It just felt so right that the role was for me. I remember a week after the interview, I was with some friends going to see a band and heard I had been invited for a second interview. I was overjoyed but my friends were less impressed because I was so distracted that I did not get ready for the gig in time!

I was informed that the second interview was to be in Birmingham the following week. I needed to see and meet the people I may be working with day to day. I drove down to Birmingham and attended the second interview. At the end of the interview, I was offered the role.

There is a Bethel song called 'Take Courage' and the lyrics of the chorus are:

*Take courage my heart,*
*Stay steadfast my soul, it's in the waiting.*

I remembered that song at that very moment and texted the lyrics to every single person who had been praying for this interview for me. It was true — He didn't fail me, and He gave me the perfect opportunity at the right time for me. I was healing before this role came along.

At the beginning of December 2017, I started my new role at Hope for Justice and the future was bright again. I was not hiding on the black leather couch, I was relaxing on it once again. I did not know then how much this role would change my life, my work and my whole existence.

I would love to take a moment to tell you a little about the work of Hope for Justice. The charity was set up in 2009 to tackle the blight that is modern day slavery. Hope for Justice works across nine countries to 'Prevent, Rescue, Restore and Reform' (the pillars of the charity) modern slavery in society. Their strapline is 'End Slavery, Change Lives'. Working from the inside as a staff member, I can honestly say I have never worked for an organisation that values its employees as much as the victims and survivors it represents. I felt truly honoured to be part of the team.

I remember on my first day having a picture taken next to the Freedom Wall and being so proud that I just couldn't wait to share it on social media. When I joined Hope for Justice, there were about thirty members of staff. Today, I think there are that number just on the senior team as it has grown a great deal. If you have read the back cover of this book, you will know that some of the proceeds will be donated to the charity.

I worked directly with survivors as part of the 'Restore' pillar of the charity. Two days a week, I would set off from home at 6:30am and return at 6:30pm. You will recall I became Dottie's human the year before, so the only solution for her was to go into doggy day-care as twelve hours was far too long for her to be alone. I remember after working with the survivors for six months, I walked into the office one day and said doggy day-care would be a great environment for survivors. The office laughed at the time, and I put the idea to one side.

Hope for Justice was, and still is, a very passionate extroverted organisation which absolutely suited my personality. I did have to solve serious legal problems, but I definitely had the personality for this organisation. In my time at Hope for Justice, I worked with about sixty survivors of modern slavery.

The thing most people won't understand is once a survivor is rescued from modern slavery in the UK, they are then persecuted by a system that requires internet literacy and good English language. During trafficking and modern slavery, victims may have their ID taken. Their traffickers often use their ID to fraudulently obtain bank accounts and take out loans, run 'crash for cash' schemes, take out credit and create other bad debts. The victim (as they still are) is blissfully unaware. When obtaining National Insurance (NI) numbers, traffickers persuade victims that they need to sign the NI numbers over to the traffickers.

Consequently, rescued survivors are usually in a situation where they have no ID, are homeless, have no form of income and are often bruised, battered and physically and emotionally exhausted. They will have been assaulted multiple times and have worked for very little income, if any. Most work at least twelve hours a day, seven days a week. Many of the trafficked workers have been in the UK long enough to gain legal citizenship but need help to claim this. You can imagine the impact this may have on someone who has had control removed in every aspect of their life.

Quite commonly, once becoming stabilised mentally and emotionally 'work ready', survivors start using their NI number again and begin receiving demands for overpayment of tax credits, debts and claims that their traffickers took out in their names. These situations can go on for years and years.

The Independent Modern Slavery Advocate helps them resolve those issues, enabling a survivor to be truly free. That was my role and it was an honour and a privilege to work for survivors...it changed my life. I had found my mission, I wanted to change lives. I wanted slavey to end and I would do pretty much anything to try and educate people on this subject. I did, and still do, find most people don't seem to want to know.

Modern slavery is ugly. People don't think about the slavery involved when they buy that bargain £1 top or those cheaper-than-expected shoes. The material alone costs more. Who on earth do people think makes these goods?

It is estimated that there is around one-hundred and thirty-six thousand people trapped in modern slavery in the UK today, with forty-million slaves worldwide.

Next time you buy cheap goods, just think about the people who have made them. My sixty clients were just a drop in the ocean! I started working for Hope for Justice at the end of 2017 and I had now finally found my mission. I felt like I was home, where God wanted me. I had finally found the legal area I had a passion for. In the meantime, my business — which was and still is my bread and butter — was growing.

At the beginning of 2018, I wanted to learn more about my faith, so started a plan to read the whole of the Bible in a year. At the same time, I took on more commitments within the church, the homeless outreach, praying for people, life group and worship team. I loved my church family and the members embraced my character and built me up. They encouraged me, prophesied over me and counselled me when the tears flowed; they never chided and criticised what I was doing and let me learn and discern on my own when things were not right. I was so blessed to be part of this amazing community. My church family was not judgemental about my choices and let me work out what was right and encouraged me along the way.

Reading and understanding the Bible and its history really assisted me in my walk of faith. For those of you reading this book who dismiss the Bible, the table below might help you understand why many people don't agree. It has been around for two-thousand years and the table represents how the Bible stacks up against other historical documents.

There are people in the world in prison, being tortured and dying because of this book. Just ask yourself: Why do government authorities want to keep people from reading this book? Ask yourself: What is so damaging that we cannot discern ourselves its contents? Why is this book banned when others are not? Could it possibly be that this book, aside from any others you know, contains something so special that governments are scared of it? No other book I have known gets this treatment.

If you look at the table below (used with kind permission from Alpha), you will see that numerous accepted scripts in history were written many years after the events. The Bible's New Testament was written only thirty to forty years after the events compare to those scripts. That is like someone my age (forty-something) writing about the 1966 World Cup: we know it happened because our parents referenced it, even though we did not witness it ourselves.

The year of reading the Bible gave me revelation about my purpose in life. Just look at the facts and ask yourselves the questions I asked earlier. Let's face it, it would be daft to dismiss something without actually reading the text. Do you do that in any other area of your life?

| WORK | WHEN WRITTEN | EARLIEST COPY | TIME LAPSE | COPIES |
|---|---|---|---|---|
| HERODOTUS | 488 - 428 BC | AD 900 | 1,300 YEARS | 8 |
| THUCYDIDES | C. 460-400 BC | C. AD 900 | 1,300 YEARS | 8 |
| TACITUS | AD 100 | AD 1100 | 1,000 YEARS | 20 |
| CAESAR'S *GALLIC WAR* | 58 - 50 BC | AD 900 | 950 YEARS | 9-10 |
| LIVY'S *ROMAN HISTORY* | 59 BC – AD 17 | AD 900 | 900 YEARS | 20 |
| NEW TESTAMENT | AD 40 – 100 | AD 130 (*Full Manuscripts AD 350*) | 30-310 YEARS | 5,000+ Greek 10,000+ Latin 9,300 others |

# End of chapter challenge

In this chapter, I shared with you how I finally discovered my mission in life. I finally discovered where I could be useful, where I felt God wanted me to be. I know not all of you who are reading this will believe in God. I believe that everyone has a plan and a purpose in life, which is more than the next big house or a new car. You can't take your wealth with you after your life ends. I believe that we're not just here to get on the treadmill of life and be sheep following others. Everyone has a mission, a particular passion for something.

My question would be: Do you know what your passion is? Do you know what your mission is? Have you identified where your strengths are? I found my passion by listening to people who inspired me. Find that person who inspires you to do more than just earn money, buy cars and own big houses. Find that person who inspires you to treat your fellow man better. Once you have found that person, start listening to them and find your passion. Pursue that passion, you will get so much more from pursuing that passion than in cars, houses and material things. You will feel fulfilled! My challenge to you is find your passion.

# Chapter 6
# Training to Climb Mountains

*"I can do all things through*
*Christ who strengthens me."*
***Philippians 4:13***

*The next moment I start to hear sounds — my arms are now hurting me. I had positioned them behind my head to protect it at every bump. I have no idea which camp we are arriving at but there's lots of chattering around me. I am feeling so much better now and am helped from the gurney and go to yet another luxurious long drop. It was a relief to be steady on my feet. No need to pray this time that I wouldn't fall in! I got back on the gurney and waited...it seemed like an age we were there. I was pondering what I would do next when back at the hotel. I was feeling so much better, my O2 measured seventy-eight percent, so everyone was able to take a rest.*

*Six of the porters were leaving the party to go and meet the rest of the team at one of the camps. I am sure walking back up the mountain would have seemed like child's play after carrying me down! I was starting to see light and hope and no longer felt my life was in the balance. The first few hours of that morning had me extremely frightened.*

*I knew, now, I was going to be OK and had peace, but it was still a frightening experience. This experience had truly changed my life...*

## Breathing More Easily Now

By the end of 2018, I had read through the whole Bible in one year. This gave me a real understanding of the faith I had first confessed to in 2012. The more I read, the more I wanted to read. I became more and more convicted about my poor behaviour regarding alcohol and tobacco. I was well known as the 'party happy drunk'. I no longer wanted to carry this reputation and the more I read about Jesus, the more I wanted to be closer to Him. Alcohol and tobacco were not the way to be closer to him — in fact the opposite. I needed to change.

I had tried to quit smoking so many times but had not succeeded. I'd heard that Allen Carr's 'Easy Way to Stop Smoking' was a good book and a good way to get rid of the filthy habit. At the time, I was driving one-hundred miles, three times a week so discovered the joy of audiobooks. I began to listen. At the beginning of the book, you are encouraged not to quit. As I went through the book, I began to hate smoking. I was nearly at the end of the book mid-January 2019.

I knew I would be challenged to stop smoking at the end of the book – three chapters left when I arrived home on the Tuesday. I still had a full pack of cigarettes and, like a typical smoker, I knew I had to finish the packet before I could attempt quitting.

I smoked like a chimney the rest of the week! When I arrived home on the Thursday, I had five cigarettes left. "Great," I thought, "Friday was quit day." I proceeded, as any non-self-respecting smoker, would and smoked my last five cigarettes.

The date was 18th January, 2019. I sat in the car to drive to work the next day. I made a quick phone call. I needed to be accountable to someone so phoned a close friend, a worship pastor at my church. I confessed that I had been secretly smoking but today was 'Quit Day'.

The next thing I did was listen to the last three chapters and that was that! The following week, I found a full packet of twenty cigarettes in a bag...I disposed of them. I was so chuffed that I managed to get rid of that full packet of cigarettes without even thinking about smoking one of them. I quit drinking altogether for a while, to give myself the best chance of remaining a non-smoker. Those of you who are reading this and smoke, will appreciate that smoking and drinking seem to go together. That was nearly three years ago and I'm still not smoking. The black leather couch is now a relaxing place, not a place to sit and smoke and drink.

If you are reading this and don't have a background in the Church or reading the Bible, I would ask you one question: How can you dismiss something you have never read or understood? In reading the Bible, it is easy to get bogged down in some of the Old Testament. I would encourage you to read the New Testament first a few times, and once you feel you understand, go back to the Old Testament. Jesus coming to fulfil the Old Testament law makes more sense that way.

---

*The six porters and my English-speaking guide left the camp with me strapped back into the gurney. I wondered how the porters had decided who would take me down and who would re-join camp. We continued our downward journey. My guide informed me that we did not have long to go before we were meeting the support vehicle for the next stage of the journey.*

*We continued down the rocky terrain. Those steps and my banging head were getting easier to work around; my hands were behind my head most of the time. My arm muscles were aching, but it was worth it to protect my head.*

*The guide was right: we soon pulled in and all the porters rested. I was instructed to get off the gurney and took a seat on a random bench — clearly the bench was there for that reason. Our transport four-by-four arrived — I think it was a Toyota — it reminded me of the series of 'Top Gear', where the team had tried to destroy a Toyota pick-up and failed.*

*I got into the passenger's side of the vehicle and sat in silence, beginning again to ponder how on earth I had arrived at this point.*

---

## Impact by Name, Impact by Nature

In February 2019, soon after I quit smoking, we were invited as a church to take part in an 'Impact Week'. It was run by a charity called Mission24 — I signed up.

The founder, Jonathan Conrathe, had preached at church once and is known in the Christian world as 'on fire for Jesus'. The only way I can describe this is that all Jonathan cares about is making sure anyone and everyone has the opportunity to know the peace and love of Jesus.

The 'Impact Week' arrived and Jonathan and his associate evangelists were equipping about sixty of us to get out of the church building and talk to people on the streets. I learned that people are often hurt by people at church (remember it is the people not the church itself that hurts). We were taught to go back to biblical principles, to strip back those principles and apply them in order to have an impact on those around us.

Jonathan described the gospel in such a simple and easy to understand way. At the end of the week, I felt equipped to have conversations with anyone about my faith and explain it. It is up to an individual whether they accept it or not. If people reject that decision, it is not for me to judge...we do not know other experiences a person may have.

I did say by the end of the week I felt equipped. This was not the case on day one. I will never forget day two of 'Impact Week': I remember exactly where I was sitting in the church building. We had already spent day one learning the simple truths about the gospel. Justin Slade (associate evangelist) began speaking. About ten minutes in, he said, 'In about twenty minutes we will be going out on the streets.' Well, if we were not awake at that point, we woke up very quickly!

I don't think I have ever seen sixty Christians try and move to the back of their chairs so quickly! We had spent the whole of the previous day learning the biblical truths about Jesus. What on earth would scare us so much? I remember feeling fear that I would offend someone. For those of you who know me, this would surprise you. On the Myers-Briggs psychometric test scale, I am an **ENFJ** with a massive capital E (extrovert), and speaking to random strangers has never been an issue. I have no idea why I feared speaking to people about my faith, but I knew in that moment I did. I was fearful. After collaborating with other people into flat refusing to go out at one point, we all summoned the courage and left the building.

I can honestly say my journey up the mountain began on day two of 'Impact Week'. Having the courage to step out and share my faith unlocked something inside of me. I find it difficult to describe, but it is best reflected by the verse at the start of this chapter — Philippians 4:13:

"I can do all things through Christ who strengthens me."

I finally believed that I could do anything — that anything was possible.

That lunchtime, once we arrived back at the church after being on the streets and chatting to people, everyone had something to share. There were stories of people who had been healed, people who had accepted the gospel message, people who had accepted prayer and lots and lots of amazing conversations. That lunchtime, there was a great buzz about the room. It is a scene I will never forget.

On the Thursday of 'Impact Week', Jonathan talked about completing a year studying with him as an intern. It piqued my interest. I had thoroughly enjoyed going onto the streets and sharing my faith, sharing this story of how reading the Bible and discovering Jesus had given me a new life, a different life, and a more amazing life than the one I had been living previously. I enjoyed sharing how my faith had convicted me to stop smoking and drink less. (I still enjoy a glass of wine but do not get drunk like I used to). I wanted to know more and wanted to be a confident evangelist.

I applied for a course which would begin in September 2019. I knew I had a mission in the world, one more fulfilling than anything I had previously done. I was healing from tragedy and I felt my life was being rebuilt. About four weeks after the 'Impact Week' came the 'Hope Conference'.

At the time, the conference was an annual event in the Hope for Justice calendar. Supporters and friends would be invited to Manchester to celebrate the past year's achievements and then be introduced to the new programmes, educating supporters about what was next. My assigned role at 'Hope Conference' was at the front door greeting everyone. I loved welcoming people, it was right up my street having to talk to complete strangers and give them a 'high five' on the way through the door.

On Saturday, 23rd March, 2019, all guests were in the building. The programmes team had shared about the various initiatives in the nine countries Hope for Justice operates in. I was particularly impacted by the children in India working in brick kilns.

Such a complex issue, these children are often the only wage earners in their family. The solution was not just economics: families would be left in poverty if their child no longer worked. It needed different collaborative solutions.

Next came pictures of Ugandan brothels. Imagine a warship and the sailors' bunks: these brothels were nothing more than this. Young children were 'living' in these small, cramped beds, one on top of another, with a curtain as privacy, at the beck and call of the next 'punter'. I can remember crying at the sight. What kind of childhood was that!

The next speaker was Tim Nelson, CEO of Hope for Justice (at the time International Development Director). Tim began speaking about an 'Extreme Challenge' to raise awareness for the charity and to raise much needed funds. Each person had to raise a minimum of £5,000 and the trip would cost another £2,700. The challenge was to climb Kilimanjaro.

I realised quickly that I had been praying for something — and that something had just landed! It was ten years since Marie had passed away. I wanted to honour her memory by turning something which impacted me negatively at the time into a positive. She was in abusive relationships and whilst not modern slavery, it is not dissimilar in its nature.

I could not think of a better tribute to my sister than raising money for Hope for Justice in her honour, creating something good out of something so rubbish.

I mean, what 45-year-old who had not exercised for twenty years, had just stopped smoking like a chimney, and had stopped drinking wouldn't sign up? After all, it was only walking up a hill — right? And why not dedicate it to Marie. I signed up.

Because 'I can do all things through Christ who strengthens me' I decided to raise £10,000 to represent the ten years since Marie had died. I had sent the email to Tim before he had even finished speaking. I found out at the beginning of May I was accepted on the team and immediately set up my fundraising page. Mountain climbing had begun! I sat down on the black leather couch and contemplated my next steps.

I decided I was going to fund myself to go on the trip so that all funds raised would go directly to the charity. Freda had to go. We had some great times together, but the funds would be enough to pay for my trip. I remember seeing Freda drive away with her new owners. They were an Aussie couple looking to tour the UK, so I knew Freda would have fun on her next journey.


## Serious Training Begins

First things first: I needed to get my backside off that black leather couch and get fit. I enrolled in the gym in May and enlisted a personal trainer to help me get fit in the right muscles. Each week, I would complete three trips to the gym coupled with outdoor hikes. It was an intense programme with three types of exercise: cardio, weights and training in the Derbyshire Peak District.

I remember doing a live social media video on a piece of cardio kit to launch my training campaign. Signed up and ready to go, I went home and sat on the black leather couch. After two minutes of cardio, I was exhausted! The thing I remember most about that training programme was the thirty minutes climbing the stairs every Friday night on the 'stair climber'. I am pretty sure I will never darken the doors of that piece of equipment again.

I also had to walk up hills, initially once a week and then twice a week. I found a great route up Back Tor, Mam Tor, Loose Hill and the Ridge, a nine-mile trek in the Peak District. When I first calculated the walk, the online guide said it would take four-and-a-half hours. I went out the first time with two friends. We set off at about 11am from Edale. We did not get back to the car until 6pm — I was slow! I remember after that first walk, I arrived home at about 8pm in the evening. Yes, I crashed! That black leather couch had never been so welcoming!

Over the weeks, the same walk got faster until I had it down to four-and-a-half hours without stopping. I enlisted the help of one or two friends to go walking with. One friend and I set out to do the Yorkshire Three Peaks one weekend. It turned out to be one of the hottest weekends in June. I was still very slow and we only managed two peaks.

After each training hike, and every so often when I achieved something new in the gym, I would sit on the black leather couch and update social media with a status including my fundraising page. I am pretty sure that people got sick of seeing my updates and donated so they could ignore them!

At the beginning of the journey, I asked a friend to print some t-shirts — you couldn't miss them! On the front and back, they had a picture of a mountain and in large letters said, 'Sheralyn's Trek to Fight Trafficking' plus the Hope for Justice logo. On the back, they also had the fundraising page. Everywhere I went for six months, it was the only t-shirt you would see me in. To reassure you, I did have four, so they were always clean!

I would tell any stranger about what I was doing and why — quite often resulting in a donation. It would not matter what situation I was in; I would see an opportunity to raise the profile of what I was doing and why. I remember one day being stuck in Manchester Piccadilly station with my train cancelled due to flooding. I remember writing a status about the many different choices I had to get around the problem: staying with friends, taxis to various locations, trains to different nearby stations, etc. It struck me how many choices I had in comparison to a victim of modern slavery. A status update was uploaded and again the fundraising effort was plugged. I lived, breathed and ate this challenge for five months, as did anyone on my social media. I may be the very reason Facebook introduced the 'unfollow' option!

One of the most significant climbs completed in training was at the end of July 2019. I had asked Charlie to accompany me due to the significance of this climb. Ten years to the day, Marie had died. After all, she was the major motivation (other than raising funds for a fantastic charity) for taking on this gargantuan task. We decided we would climb Snowdon.

We set out just after breakfast to climb Snowdon and the weather was glorious. We had all the kit we needed and enough snacks to sink a battleship. Well, not quite, but lots.

We began the walk up the Pyg track. All was looking well until about halfway up. The heavens opened and it rained and rained — and rained some more. Clouds were closing in and we lost the view of the top of the peak of Snowdon. We struggled on! I had written a speech to video at the top of Snowdon to explain fully what I was doing and why I had chosen this challenge in this particular year.

We finally got to the top of Snowdon at about five in the afternoon and were both shattered. In the weather conditions, it had required a herculean effort. We sat in the café and recovered with Dottie, who by then was shivering. I stood in the entrance of the café and shared my video — we were exhausted. We needed to get the train back. I enquired at the café for tickets; we could get on the train, Dottie could not.

Charlie, bless him, offered to walk down again with Dottie and a couple of folks we had just met. I would get the train, find a lift to my car, and then meet them at the bottom and give the newfound friends a lift to their car. I was very thankful! I took a ticket and my place on the train. On the way down, I was blessed to meet a family who offered to give me a lift back to my car. I arrived at the car park and waited for Charlie and his newfound friends plus Dottie to emerge. We eventually set off home and arrived back at about midnight, Dottie slept the whole way.

No time to collapse on the black leather couch, I collapsed on the bed!

Not only did I badger everyone I came across to sponsor me, I also organised two events. The first was a fun day. There were five people in the small 'Abolition Group' and we prayed lots. I needed all of them to help on this day. We chose a date and worked towards the given date. It was the first time I had organised anything of this magnitude. We brainstormed ideas for things to do and ended up with 'Pelt-a-Pastor', a bouncy castle, outdoor games and a geocache — a kind of GPS based hide-and-seek. Indoors, we had a hall to sell cakes, coffee, crafts and honey. I should not have been surprised when people jumped on board! Pastors agreed to be pelted, cakes were pledged, volunteers were enlisted (about thirty) and the day was set.

One minor snag was the weather. The summer of 2019 was very wet: day after day after day it rained. We prayed and prayed and prayed. The day before was awful, so we prayed some more. Much to our delight, our prayers were answered: the weather was glorious, the pastors, volunteers, customers and all the cakes showed up! We raised over £900 on the day in £1 and £2 amounts. Phenomenal! I needed a rest on the black leather couch after that.

The second event was a 'Concert of Hope'. It was timed for a 'Hope Sunday' and the amazing church choir agreed to take part to support me. Again, it was total answer to prayer. We raised an amazing £1,200 on the night.

These two events boosted my total so much. At the time of setting off for the mountain, I had raised £7,200. Now, all I had to do was climb the mountain.

# End of Chapter Challenge

Think about something you want to achieve that you believe is impossible. Draw two columns: one column sets out the reasons you are equipped to achieve the impossible the other states the reasons that stop you from committing to achieve the impossible task. Go through each of the negative reasons and solve the problem.

If you are fearful of something, you see barriers where they don't exist. Don't make assumptions about anything, only assess the information and facts you have. A common human failing relates to having conversations with other people in our head. We imagine what they are going to say, how they are going to react and what they are going to do when presented with our plan. Before we even start, we allow those 'in our head' conversations to talk us out of our plans or, even worse, approach the actual conversations with friends and family negatively. I used to think like that. After the 'Impact Week' and 'Hope Conference' this had changed. I had a belief that, 'I can do all things through Christ who strengthens me.'

And He did.

# COUCH TO KILIMANJARO

SHERALYN PATTISON

# Chapter 7
# The Climb

*I lift up my eyes to the mountains —*
*where does my help come from?*
*My help comes from the Lord,*
*the Maker of heaven and earth.*
*He will not let your foot slip —*
*he who watches over you will not slumber;*
*indeed, he who watches over Israel*
*will neither slumber nor sleep.*
*The Lord watches over you —*
*the Lord is your shade at your right hand;*
*the sun will not harm you by day,*
*nor the moon by night.*
*The Lord will keep you from all harm —*
*he will watch over your life;*
*the Lord will watch over your coming and going*
*both now and forevermore.*
**Psalm 121 (NIV)**

*As we continued to descend in the vehicle, I started to look around and could see the porters' clothing. One shirt caught my eye: it was green and white with long green sleeves and a white body. There were holes on the wrists, it looked like it had been used at some point for makeshift gloves. Another shirt was a Manchester United top: the imprint was nearly worn out and, again, at the edges there were holes. We were told a lot of the porters did not have good gloves. When it came to the end of the trip, we were given the opportunity to donate clothing to the porters. Ernie, one of the other climbers, arranged for it all to be laundered. It seemed such a small thing and something we all responded to. It was good to know that we left an item there that would do good. It reminded me we were in the developing world, something which had come into sharp focus six days previously...*

---

## At the Airport

The time had come: after months of training and fundraising, time to climb mountains. On 22nd October, 2019 I headed to Heathrow to meet some of my fellow climbers for the first time and to begin what would be a life-changing adventure. We were initially flying to Ethiopia to see some of the children's 'Lighthouses' which Hope for Justice runs for survivors. I had been working with survivors for years. I was aware of the need for funds I knew who I was climbing for — or so I thought. It was exciting to meet new folk.

There had a been a few online communications prior to the trip. The twenty-two of us came from so many different locations: Manchester, London, East Midlands, Belgium, Ibiza, Utah, Texas, Alabama, Florida. With that mix, it was impossible to meet face to face before the trip. A few of us met for the first time at Heathrow. It was so exciting. I remember being by the departure board and taking a picture with all my stuff...we were off!

It was a good flight to Ethiopia. We had been advised to wear our walking boots on the journey. Our hand luggage should also carry at least two days' worth of clothing should our luggage not arrive. Quite commonly, luggage doesn't make it through to Ethiopia at the airport. I had put two luggage bags in the hold; one had all the team merchandise in. When we landed in Ethiopia, I was desperate to check whether the merchandise had arrived — so desperate that I left my hand luggage in the overhead locker. I didn't realise till I had gone through passport control and was at baggage reclaim. The hand luggage had Marie's picture in...she nearly didn't make it to the bottom of the mountain. After a fractious thirty-minute wait at baggage reclaim, the hand luggage was retrieved...phew! Marie would make it up the mountain!

We arrived at the hotel and settled into rooms. A few of us arranged to meet up and go for some dinner. Hunter, Greg, Harriet and I decided to go for traditional Ethiopian cuisine. Greg and Hunter had completed a guided tour round the city in the afternoon and they arranged with their driver to take us to a traditional Ethiopian restaurant. A few of us ordered the traditional cuisine. What arrived was a large circular platter.

In the centre were a selection of various meaty spicy dishes. Around the outside, arranged in a pretty fashion, was traditional injera bread. The bread is made from teff flour and water and risen to give a sponge-like consistency. The first time we ate it, it was pleasant but as the days went on, it became known as 'endurance' bread. It seemed tasteless but was clearly enjoyed by the locals.

On day two in Ethiopia, we visited the boy's 'Lighthouse'. We had the opportunity to meet some of the children and staff at the house. Arriving with some trepidation, the boys were fascinated by our visit, and we toured round the classrooms and living quarters. It was so humbling to see all these children. Only months earlier, they were on the streets, something we would get to see first-hand later. Their stories were similar: quite often, their families were poor, and someone (a trafficker) had come to the village. The trafficker had offered a 'better life' with education for the child. Parents had thought they were sending their children to good prospects. Instead, the children would end up working relentlessly long hours with little or no pay and no education. Inevitably, when slave masters no longer wanted their services, they would end up on the streets of Addis Ababa.

These children had been befriended by outreach workers on the streets and then invited to the 'Lighthouse' for hope, education and a future — it was just wonderful being there. We played basketball and had lunch. After lunch, Greg taught us all a new game, Four Square. It was beautiful playing games with some very happy children who had been through more than any child should in their young lives.

It was great to see the smiles and genuine happiness and joy at being somewhere safe. 'Hope for Justice

Lighthouses' help the children recover through a programme of therapy and education. Their family is often successfully located and children are reunited with parents.

In the evening, we went on a trip that I will never forget. We all piled into our minibus and headed off into Addis Ababa. After a short time, we were driving down a street where every five yards we would see street children who had either already been prey to traffickers or were going to be prey for traffickers. Hope for Justice outreach workers work on these streets distributing food and drinks and engaging with the children. The first street seemed at least two miles long and there were groups of children standing every few yards from one another, some sleeping on the ground, too — hundreds and hundreds of boys.

The next street distressed me the most. The street was similar size in length and was adjacent to the one where all the male street children were located. I did not expect to see what we saw. Every five to ten yards was a young girl; some looked age ten or eleven, or younger. Some were slightly older than that. Every shop doorway had a little girl standing there, scantily clad waiting for trade to pass. At every fourth or fifth shop were a group of adult men and some older girls with lights, music and a bar — brothels.

This street went on and on. There were so many young girls. As we were driving, you could have heard a pin drop in the minibus, we were all stunned into silence at what we were seeing. I was moved to tears and even as I write, it has bought me to tears again.

If I needed any more motivation to climb a mountain, there it was.

Prevention and rescue of these young boys and girls must be a top priority. In all my work with survivors, I don't think I have ever been impacted so much by one single event as I was that day. We arrived back at the hotel and I was so distressed, I did not want to go straight to my room. Tim sat with me – he helped me see how many lives would be impacted by the funds I had raised so far.

The day before we began our journey up Kilimanjaro, we travelled to Tanzania and met the rest of our fellow climbers. The hotel was lovely and after all the build-up, it was great to meet the team. We completed a team briefing and went to pack our holdalls ready for the climb the next day. I remember I had far too much stuff and had to seriously reduce it. Too many socks, too many sweaters... well too much of everything! The following morning, we were excited and apprehensive. There was an amazing view of Kilimanjaro from the hotel. Such a distinctive mountain with what looked like a flat top. It is easy to see from this distance why it is called the Rooftop of Africa.

All twenty-two of us met in the lobby with our holdalls plus day bags. Such anticipation! The minibus was an old, rickety one and I remember thinking, "This bus doesn't look like it will get us to the end of the road, never mind any further!" I didn't voice this concern as we were so excited to finally be on our way.

We piled into the rickety bus and began our journey uphill. Along the way I sat next to one of my fellow climbers, David Trombly (T Bone). He shared his amazing background. T Bone is a cancer survivor from a rare lymphoma which no one in the US military had ever survived beyond 5 years after diagnosis. Nineteen years previously, he had been given two years to live, and here he was sitting next to me on this bus, now cancer free and telling the tale. He was a retired US Marine fighter pilot. I was captivated by his story; he has captured this in his book 'Grounded and Cured'. T Bone was a real encouragement to me from the outset – I was soon to learn how invaluable it was having him stand next to me when climbing that mountain. If you are thinking of climbing a mountain, see if you can enlist a retired US Marine fighter pilot to assist. Invaluable!

---

*The support vehicle comes to a halt. The place looks familiar; I am back at Machame Gate. I look at the guard station. A medic joins me in the back of the vehicle. The oximeter is placed on my finger and my O2 is back up to a very normal ninety-six percent with my resting heart rate down a regular seventy-five. The medic asked me whether I would like to go to hospital. My cheeks were buzzing but I felt completely normal.*

*I was more desperate to get back to the hotel and have my first shower in six days than go and sit in a stiflingly hot hospital. I declined the offer. The support vehicle started and as we headed through the gate. As I looked left, there was the shelter we were under six days previously.*

---

## Let the Climbing Commence...

We arrived at Machame Gate and our amazing photographers and videographers, Tom Harmer and Dominic Magdalena, took individual and team pictures to document the moment. Not only did these two legends film and take pictures along the way, but they also completed the climb — the only reason there are any halfway decent photos of me taking part in this challenge is down to them! The trek leader was Tim Nelson. I have never known anyone who can multitask quite so successfully and still 'be there' when you are speaking to him. He looked after our health individually and collectively, filmed various videos, carried essential supplies and sponsorship materials and got to know us really well.

We set off together and that first day was amazing. I was at the front of the pack, singing along and kept a good pace. One of my favourite moments on that day was trekking and singing 'Praise the name of the Lord Our God'. It was great to be there. I think my fellow climbers appreciated my vocal efforts both on day one and throughout the climb (like a hole in the head).

That first night, I started to feel a bit peaky. Mr Delicious managed to cook some of the greatest food you could imagine on a mountain. I think the firm favourite for everyone was the shepherd's pie pizza on summit night. After that first night, though, I ate very little of his delights as I was feeling so rough from day two onwards. I had taken a supply of protein shakes to keep up my protein intake for the arduous trek and climb, a Godsend, in hindsight.

Day two began. We had to be packed and ready to go at 6:30am every day. Our luggage would be grouped together in large bags, and we would go for breakfast. Next to the mess tent was a clean supply of water for each of us to fill up with the requisite three litres of water needed for the trek. We would sit down and have our O2 stats recorded. That morning, my O2 registered at ninety-five per cent saturation with my pulse at ninety-five bpm. Just before sitting down at the breakfast table, I felt very ill but forced myself to have something to eat.

After breakfast, I began to feel dizzy and vomited twice — I felt rough. I do not know whether you can imagine this feeling: the day involves a trek uphill of five kilometres and increasing altitude another three-thousand feet, you have a bout of what you think is sickness and diarrhoea, and you are feeling breathless with no energy. Well, that was start of day two. I began the trek but quickly had to stop. I was struggling — going back was not an option, I had already raised £7,200 and wanted to raise the other £2,800 to make that £10,000. That ten-year mark was so important to me.

I needed to achieve my target total and create something good out of the, quite frankly, rubbish reality that we had lost a sister ten years ago.

If you ever have a moment like this, it would be great to have on hand a newly retired US Marine fighter pilot, a Director of an international charitable foundation and a construction business owner from Texas. Fortunately for me, I did indeed have T Bone, Greg Larsen and Tod Tracy! As soon as they saw me struggling, they stopped and checked in. There was nothing truer than Psalm 121 for me that day — 'I lift up my eyes to the mountains, where does my help come from? My help comes from the Lord' — in the form of T Bone, Greg and Tod.

I told them to carry on and leave me to it, I knew it was going to be a slow day for me and I would keep them back from the main group — I really didn't want to be a burden. They were having none of it and insisted they would trek with me. I was so thankful in that moment and remain so. I truly believe I would not have made it to the end of that day or beyond if it had not been for the three of them. I recently confirmed as much, the chief guide would have shipped me off but for my three helpers that day.

We set out together and I was slow. I felt like we were stopping every five yards for a rest, they had so much patience. It began to rain. Soon enough, it was pouring with rain. I very quickly gave up on carrying my own bag and the porters carried this for me. The four of us were accompanied by four guides. It was horribly wet, there were waterfalls everywhere and scrambling was the only possible way to pass up the trail.

There were many times when Greg had my hand pulling me up rocks and T Bone was pushing me from behind.

The porters thought I would give up that day but towards the latter part of the day kept commenting in Swahili that they knew I was never going to give up. That day, I truly overcame adversity with the help the Lord provided. We overcame the weather, waterfalls, the climb, the terrain, absolutely everything, and finally made it to camp about three hours after everyone else. I still felt rough. I had hot water and a protein shake for tea and then went to bed.

My O2 measured at eighty-two percent and heart rate measured one-hundred-and-two bpm.

I woke up on day three feeling much better. I began to sing 'Raise a Hallelujah', much to the delight (at least that's what I think those faces were) of my fellow climbers. I was singing this to rev myself up more than anything. Going back down was still not an option – I was going to keep trekking so long as I could physically move. My O2 that morning was eighty-five per cent with a pulse at ninety-six bpm.

Day three was acclimatisation day: we would walk up to Lava Tower and then descend back down to the camp at the bottom of Burranco Wall. I set off for the uphill trek of seven kilometres followed by a downward trek of three kilometres. Again, my trek was slow and I was accompanied by the amazing gent that is Geoff Chad. At the time, Geoff was 71. He is a retired pastor and was such a patient and graceful gent all day. I stopped every five minutes it seemed. It took us three more hours than everyone else to get to the lunch stop.

The landscape at this point on Kilimanjaro is grey rock and more grey rock, so a lot of chatting was done to pass the time. After the 3pm lunch there was the three-kilometre descent back to Burranco camp. This all started off relatively well but very quickly the daylight started to fade. The terrain was extremely rocky, the kind of rocks that would break your ankles with one slip. As the light faded, it dawned on the two of us that we had no head torches. We had expected to be in camp by then. The darkness was a challenge; the bigger challenge came when it began to rain, too.

In the pitch black and with wet rocky terrain, we finally descended into Burranco camp and through to the mess tent — we were received by the biggest cheer I have ever been so honoured to receive from our fellow climbers. They had all stayed in the tent as they were concerned for our welfare. This was an amazing team to be part of! As we sat down, Tim revealed what was one of my personal highlights of the whole Kilimanjaro trip. Tim and the Hope for Justice team had, prior to our trip, written to each of our emergency contacts. The team had requested a letter to encourage us, being given to us at some point in our journey — letters from home. Our fellow climbers had received their letters over dinner. As Geoff and I arrived later, ours were handed to us just after we had walked into our hero's welcome.

As Tim told me about the notes, I think I remember him saying, 'If you didn't know you were loved, you will now!'. He was right.

He shared that day after day, new notes kept arriving at Hope for Justice head office for me: he handed me forty-seven notes (one had about thirty quotes on it) from people who wanted to encourage me. I could not believe it. It was such an emotional moment! It turned out that almost sixty people from my home church plus my family had written passages of encouragement. I think Psalm 121 and Philippians 4:13 — 'I can do all things through Christ who strengthens me' — were quoted at least thirty times in these notes. If God wanted me to get a message, it came through loud and clear that night. I was loved and part of God's great family. I was totally overwhelmed. If there was a moment when I was flagging after that on the mountain, I would go back to those notes.

Day four arrived; I was petrified. Day four on the Machame route is Burranco Wall day. The evening before that trek, I had asked T Bone to help me up Burranco Wall. Burranco Wall is a non-technical but steep nine-hundred feet high cliff. I am not so good with heights and had been dreading that day from the moment I had signed up for the 'Extreme Challenge'. If you are struggling on a mountain, it is always handy to have a recently retired US Marine fighter pilot on hand to assist!

My O2 saturation that morning was at a low seventy-eight per cent. I think the lead guide was getting concerned but I was allowed to continue. I was not eating well and protein shakes were keeping me climbing. We set off and, thankfully for T Bone, I was no longer being physically ill. The sheer drop as we got higher and higher made this trek and scramble very hard for me. At points, I remember being totally petrified.

There were only a few of those moments and, thankfully, the path was clearly marked. I tried not to look over the edge.

I'd managed the climb.

The trek on the desolate rocky wasteland continued and T Bone just continued to support me getting there. We arrived at camp about two-and-a-half hours after everyone else. I saw Tim as I entered camp and I just began singing 'Raise a Hallelujah'. He turned round, and we hugged – I was so happy to be back in camp again. I will never forget the scene of Greg and some of my fellow climbers coming out of the mess tent towards me to help. I just felt so relieved and so glad to have completed the

Burranco Wall. Everyone else absolutely loved Burranco Wall — I was not so enamoured!

The terrain now was very rocky with little trail visible. This was the night where Dominic took the most amazing picture of the skyline: it was a clear, starry night and the only light pollution was the town of Moshi below. Again, I didn't eat much food that night (sorry Mr Delicious) and my O2 was back up to eight per cent. I clearly wasn't acclimatising too well and was suffering physically as a result. I was trekking two or three hours longer than everyone else the entire time.

At the start of day five, after a wonderful night's sleep, Dominic took a great picture of me thanking God with Kilimanjaro peak in the background. I was still feeling rubbish but was singing. I think this might have come across as quite bonkers, but it really was my way of motivating myself. If I am totally honest, I hated camping on the mountain,

I found the trek much tougher than I'd anticipated and it had not even occurred to me that altitude would be an issue. Underneath all the smiles and singing was someone who was just wanting to get through another day.

Day five really was my 'pole, pole' (slowly, slowly in Swahili) day. Day five is the longest day on the Machame route. The trek starts in the morning and the idea is to get to camp at midday and then rest until teatime, have tea and then rest till 11pm before starting out for the summit, which is reached as dawn breaks the following morning. This is the only safe time to be at Uhuru peak as the ground underfoot is too treacherous. The heat of the day begins, the sun melts the snow on the peak and the ground underfoot becomes unstable.

I remember on the morning of day five, T Bone came up to me. He stood directly in front of me and squared me in the face — I was little taken aback but he had my attention. He said, 'You know girl I love your energy and your enthusiasm but right now you need to come, sit down and shut up.' It was abrupt but I wasn't quite sure why. He had either heard a conversation or had figured with my O2 being so low, my onward trek was in jeopardy, and I needed to beat the oximeter. I sat down for ten minutes taking very deep breaths and not speaking (I know my fellow climbers were surprised that T Bone had managed to shut me up!). My O2 was measured, and I came in at ninety-two per cent. Lots of cheering followed and off we set. (I found out later that the guides and porters were not so impressed with T Bone for this, however.)

I was still struggling and set off with my guides. The whole group had to go ahead as the guides were working out in what order we would summit. It was quite clear I would set off first, being the slowest, so no competition there. It was an extremely 'pole pole' trek for me of six hours (everyone else did it in three). The scenery at this point on Kilimanjaro is quite desolate and rocky. By this point on the trek, I was only looking down following the purple and black gators of my guide. I was concentrating on putting one foot in front of the other. I remember thinking about Moses and feeling sorry for him. He had to climb Mount Sinai twice to get the Ten Commandments — imagine having to do this twice!

I arrived at base camp, fifteen thousand feet up at 3pm! I was totally and utterly exhausted. By then, everyone else was sleeping — exactly what I wanted. I went to bed in the tent. I wanted to stay there...it was the comfiest I had felt on the entire a trip. I'm a glamper, not a camper. The idea of a tent fills me with dread. It did the day I arrived on Kilimanjaro and it still does today.

Sadly, I had to get up for my tea and final O2 check before attempting the summit. My O2 was back down at eighty-four per cent. I was tired but still managed to bring a smile to Tim's face when I turned up wearing my balaclava. This piece of head gear had been purchased as advised to protect my ears from the cold. My original choice hadn't arrived in time for the trip so I had to improvise and this balaclava was the next best thing. Sadly, the balaclava did make me look like I was ready to jump out of a cannon! This caused much hilarity in the mess tent. We had supper and then went back off to bed.

It was decided that I would set off for the summit three hours before everyone else due to my speed. This meant just two hours rest for me. In total, I had four hours rest between arriving at base camp and attempting to summit the mountain. I have to say that when I was awoken at 8:30pm, I felt miserable. I was beyond exhausted and had just about managed to get this far. I dressed and assembled with my two guides at the mess tent. It was dark, wet, cold, snowy. The ankle breaking rocks awaited. This was the most miserable I had felt the entire time I was on the mountain. There was no singing in camp as I left, and Ben came and prayed with me. I felt like rubbish but I wanted to conquer that mountain!

I continued trekking, remembering Psalm 121 and Philippians 4:13 — I could do this! I did not want to let down all those people who had written to me, encouraged me and sponsored me on this journey. I dreamt about sitting on the black leather couch. After having a serious talk to myself, we continued up the mountain. The guides pulled me up where they could; the terrain was awful. I trekked, scrambled and kept going. But I was really struggling. I remember scrambling up a rock, slipping and sitting down exhausted. I am guessing the guides had seen someone unwell so many times on this mountain. My guide ripped off my glove and took my O2. It was sixty-five per cent. He warmed my hands and so did I.

We stretched my fingers, I felt terrible. Alone. Afraid.

In that moment, I remember thinking for the second time in my life since Mum had died, 'I want my mum.'

The guide took my O2 saturation again and there was no change. He said to me, 'Sheralyn, the mountain will always be here; you will not if we continue.' Strangely enough, I agreed. He took the decision that it was no longer safe for me to continue, and we trekked back to base camp.

As I arrived back at camp, the mess tent was full. 'Great,' I thought, 'I could see everyone before they set off for their summit attempt.' T Bone was there to hug me. It is so common in the military to honour the fallen at poignant moments. There was only one man for the job of making sure Marie would summit the mountain! T Bone carefully placed Marie's photograph secure in the pages of his manuscript. The team set off and I went back to my tent. I heard afterwards that they were quite relieved that I had arrived back at camp before they set off. They all commented how awful it would have been to see me coming down as they were going up.

My guide measured my O2 again: sixty-three per cent. There had been no recovery at all, and my guide was starting to get concerned. It was the middle of the night and pitch black. I returned to my tent and lay down. I was exhausted and defeated; I was feeling awful and was hoping and praying I would make the morning.

It felt that bad.

I can still see the tent now: I was alone in our camp; I couldn't hear any guides or porters and I knew my O2 was low. I cried until I fell to sleep. I'm not sure what time it was when I awoke but my guide was measuring my O2 again. Still sixty-three per cent.

He left me and said I needed to get dressed and he would be back again in thirty minutes. Yet another measurement! It was the same. Everything zapped my energy; I had a massive headache and was struggling to breathe. I felt like I was drunk. I described how I felt and I can remember what the guide said as clear as if it was yesterday: 'We need to get you off this mountain!' I agreed. He instructed me to pack everything as quickly as possible and meet him at the mess tent. Again, he measured my O2, there was no change — we were in dangerous territory.

We began to trek down to the emergency station. It had taken five days to get up there and took just four-and-a-half hours to get back down. I am very grateful for the swift way the porters took me off the mountain. They were quick and it was a bumpy ride The few dollars tip I gave them didn't seem enough for saving my life. Apparently, it was a couple of days wages equivalent. I don't think I have ever been so grateful to be at sea level than I was that day. Once we were down the mountain, my O2 was measured again. It was back up to a more normal ninety-six per cent.

That wasn't the end of the story though! There was still money to raise. You will recall that I said my total was only £7,200 when I started to climb Kilimanjaro. After arriving back at Machame gate, I was driven back to the hotel. I was disappointed by then that I had not made it to the summit. I was feeling very low and needed to do something to cheer me up. I contacted Hope for Justice HQ and let them know I had finished early, why I had and then said I would share later publicly.

I was most disappointed that I had not raised the £10,000 to represent the ten years after Marie's death. I took the photo of me smiling on the gurney and put up a post on social media. Within minutes, I was receiving messages of support and people urging me to continue the fundraising effort.

I decided that I would write to each of my individual contacts on social media and ask them to consider sponsoring me very early on in the challenge. When I set off to climb Kilimanjaro, I was only up to the letter C. I compiled a video of the photographs and the experience, and then added that to the individual messages. I suggested a donation and many people gave that or more.

Just before Christmas, my total was over £9,000. I kept praying and kept reaching out. I had finally reached the end of the alphabet by Christmas and was only a few hundred pounds short of my target. 'Shezza's Shower Singathon' was aired on the social media channels for one night only — thankfully.

Within ten minutes the world had decided they needed to donate to shut me up! Target reached and much relief all round...especially from the social media channels! I posted on social media that it was finally complete. It was really fitting that the target was reached the night before I was to leave for Rwanda with Mission24 for my first international mission with them. If I had not stepped out with Mission24 I do not believe I would have had the courage to step out onto that mountain. I thanked the Lord. God had given me the ability to achieve something I would never have thought possible.

Over the course of nine months, I was able to honour a much beloved sister, set out to climb a mountain and raise £10,000 for an amazing charity.

I truly had gone from Couch to Kilimanjaro.

# End of Chapter challenge

In this book, I have shared how my life went through many storms and I can empathise and sympathise with anyone who is experiencing sudden grief, divorce or contemplating whether life is worth continuing. To each and every one of you reading this, I would say that no matter what your belief system, 'YOU ARE SPECIAL, YOU ARE LOVED AND YOU WERE CREATED FOR A SPECIAL PURPOSE.

You have also read about how I was motivated to come from a very dark place to a place of triumph and light. I now look at life and instead of thinking, 'Why?' I think, 'Why not, let's try it and see?' You can have that faith too if you want it. It is a totally personal choice. You can freely receive that gift. I can recommend it. Rather than living my life with restrictions and being a slave to things, I am now living my life in freedom.

To gain that faith, why not start by praying a simple prayer? This prayer involves acknowledging that you have gone your own way in life, recognising that Jesus died on the cross for you and that you want Him to be a part of your life. It doesn't matter who you are or what you have or haven't done, or what you have been through, Jesus will accept you as you are.

If you want that acceptance, pray this prayer:

*Jesus, I want to know you more and I acknowledge up till now, I have gone my own way and not the way you intended. I am sorry.*

*Jesus, I believe in you and I want to thank you for dying on the Cross for me, please forgive me for everything I have done wrong.*

*Please come into my life and fill me with your Holy Spirit.*

*Thank you Lord.*

*Amen.*

If you have just prayed that prayer, I would love to hear from you. At the back of this book are contact details, so you can get in touch. It would be great to help you find the next steps, wherever you are in this world.

If you don't feel you can pray that prayer or don't want to as you are struggling to believe, why not challenge God? Pray and ask Him to show Himself if He is real; to reveal himself to you. This challenge comes with a caveat though: don't be surprised when something dramatic and unexplainable happens. Remember, you read these words and you prayed that prayer!

In the back of this book, are some useful links to resources which can help you explore the Christian faith more as well as any of the other books and references that are mentioned in this book. If you have got to this point in the book, I am sad to say that it is the end of this journey and now I am off to have a rest and relax!

On the black leather couch. Of course!

**COUCH TO KILIMANJARO**

SHERALYN PATTISON

# Prologue

Since writing this book, I have been inspired to climb another mountain. This time a metaphorical one rather than a physical one.

Ten years ago, when I accepted Jesus into my heart, I would never have imagined that I would be running a successful legal business. Running the legal business has given me the confidence to start a business which aligns with my passion and mission to impact the lives of those trapped in modern slavery. My love of dogs and their therapeutic effect on me have inspired me to start a business to employ survivors of modern slavery. You may remember the thought shared in this book after about six months of working for Hope for Justice. This thought is now becoming a reality.

Woofterful® Doggy Daycare will be trading by the end of 2022 in Derby. The aim of the service will be to provide a service for dogs needing day care in addition to providing employment opportunities to help traumatised survivors of modern slavery. This project is a mountain to me! The location of the centre, at the time of writing this book, is a field with nothing in it. Building the infrastructure, after obtaining the relevant planning permissions, is totally new. It is so different to anything I have done before. A major challenge. To say it will be trading by the end of 2022 is stepping out in faith. Just look out for the next book 'It's a Woofterful® Life'. I'm not sure what will be shared in it but it will most definitely be an adventure!

I do hope this book has inspired you to think about stepping off the couch and climbing your own personal mountain; the time is now.

SHERALYN PATTISON

# About the Author

Sheralyn Pattison qualified as a paralegal lawyer in 2014 and runs her own non-reserved legal business, Derby Legal Assistance. In addition to building her legal business, Sheralyn worked as an advocate for Hope for Justice, where she found her passion and mission to end trafficking and support modern slavery survivors. Sheralyn's legal business is now her 'tent making' equivalent so she can pursue her passion. Sheralyn fights many injustices on a personal level doing pro bono legal work for those in need, again supported by the legal business.

Sheralyn has started a new business, Woofterful® Ltd, trading as Woofterful® Doggy Daycare and Woofterful® Tails. The aim is to employ survivors of modern slavery to a point of full recovery in a doggy daycare setting. Survivors will be given time and support to live in full independence with hope and self-development prospects.

Sheralyn is a Trustee for two trusts: Jacob's Well and Elvaston Castle and Gardens Trust. She is a Christian evangelist and volunteers as frequently as she can with Mission24. She is an active member of New Life Church, Derby where she is a Home Church Pastor.

Sheralyn lives at home with her nephew, Charlie. Dottie dog has now been joined by Doris who is another cockapoo and just over twelve months old. One of Doris's favourite past times is terrorising Dottie and the cats called Hope (girl) and Justice (boy). Sheralyn travels as often as she can in her new caravan, Ruby, and takes Dottie and Doris on all her adventures.

# SHERALYN PATTISON

# Appendix

## Exploring Christianity More

### New Life Church Derby
https://newlifederby.org.uk/
office@newlifederby.org.uk
Tel: 01332 349056

### Alpha
https://alpha.org/about/
uk@alpha.org
Phone +44 (0)2070 520200

### Mission24
https://www.mission24.co.uk/
Phone: +44(0)1778 487267
Email: info@mission24.co.uk

### All Nations
https://allnations.org.uk/wolverhampton
Tel: 01902 714 469
Email: info@allnations.org.uk

### Derby City Vision
https://www.derbycityvision.org/

SHERALYN PATTISON

# Organisations Mentioned in This Book That Can Help And Support You

## Places for support with debt

- Jubilee Project at Derby City Mission for those local to Derby - 01332 460346,  https://www.derbycitymission.org.uk/Pages/Category/jubilee,

- Christians Against Poverty – 0800 328 000, https://capuk.org

- Money Advice Service - https://www.moneyhelper.org.uk

## Places for support with alcohol addiction

- Celebrate recovery - https://www.celebraterecovery.co.uk,

- Alcoholics Anonymous - 0800 9177 650, https://www.alcoholics-anonymous.org.uk

- Teen Challenge – 01664 822221  http://www.teenchallenge.org.uk/index.php

- Carpenters Arms – 01509 767550, https://www.carpenters-arms.org/

- Walk Ministries - 01782 870196, https://walkministries.org.uk/

- Green Pastures - https://www.greenpastures.net

## Places for support with domestic abuse

- Women's Work, Derby - 01332 242 525, https://www.womens-work.org.uk

- England – Refuge's National Domestic Abuse Helpline, 0808 2000 247, https://www.refuge.org.uk

- Northern Ireland - Domestic and Sexual Abuse Helpline, 0808 802 1414, https://www.dsahelpline.org

- Scotland - Domestic Abuse and Forced Marriage Helpline, 0800 027 1234 https://www.sdafmh.org.uk/en/

- Wales - Live Fear Free, 0808 80 10 800, https://www.welshwomensaid.org.uk/what-we-do/live-fear-free-helpline/

- UK-wide - The Men's Advice Line run by Respect is a confidential helpline specifically for male victims, 0808 801 0327, https://mensadviceline.org.uk

## Great organizations to turn to if you are struggling with mental health.

- Premier Lifeline – 0300 111 0101, https://www.premierlifeline.org.uk/who-we-are

- Samaritans – 116123, https://www.samaritans.org/how-we-can-help/contact-samaritan/

- MIND - https://www.mind.org.uk/need-urgent-help/

# Connect With Us

Throughout his book, the pictures of the experience shared can be found on the Couch to Kilimanjaro Facebook page.

You can also connect and share your experiences of the book.

https://www.facebook.com/Couch-to-Kilimanjaro

Email: couchtokilimanjaro@yahoo.co.uk

Printed in Great Britain
by Amazon

10243669R00088